Gerontological Social Work With Families
A Guide to Practice Issues and Service Delivery

The *Journal of Gerontological Social Work* series:

•*Gerontological Social Work Practice in Long-Term Care*, edited by George S. Getzel and M. Joanna Mellor

•*A Healthy Old Age: A Sourcebook for Health Promotion with Older Adults (Revised Edition)*, by Stephanie FallCreek and Molly Mettler

•*The Uses of Reminiscence: New Ways of Working with Older Adults*, edited by Marc Kaminsky

•*Gerontological Social Work in Home Health Care*, edited by Rose Dobrof

•*Gerontological Social Work Practice in the Community*, edited by George S. Getzel and M. Joanna Mellor

•*Social Work and Alzheimer's Disease: Practice Issues With Victims and Their Families*, edited by Rose Dobrof

•*Ethnicity and Gerontological Social Work*, edited by Rose Dobrof

•*Gerontological Social Work With Families: A Guide to Practice Issues and Service Delivery*, edited by Rose Dobrof

Gerontological Social Work With Families
A Guide to Practice Issues and Service Delivery

Rose Dobrof
Editor

The Haworth Press
New York • London

Gerontological Social Work With Families: A Guide to Practice Issues and Service Delivery has also been published as *Journal of Gerontological Social Work*, Volume 10, Numbers 1/2, January 1987.

The Haworth Press, Inc., 12 West 32 Street, New York, NY 10001
EUROSPAN/Haworth, 3 Henrietta Street, London WC2E 8LU England

Library of Congress Cataloging-in-Publication Data

Gerontological social work with families.

Published also as v. 10, nos. 1/2, January 1987, of the Journal of gerontological social work.
Includes bibliographies.
1. Social work with the aged—United States. 2. Aged—Services for—United States. 3. Aged—United States—Family relationships. 4. Aged—Care and treatment—United States. I. Dobrof, Rose.
HV1461.G49   1986   362.6′042   86-14930
ISBN 0-86656-599-X

Gerontological Social Work With Families

A Guide to Practice Issues and Service Delivery

Journal of Gerontological Social Work
Volume 10, Numbers 1/2

CONTENTS

FROM THE EDITOR   1

**Social Work Practice With Family Systems in Admission
to Homes for the Aged**   5
Marion Bogo, MSW, AdvDipSW

Introduction   5
Family Involvement With the Elder   6
Family Therapy and Gerontology   7
Family Systems Theory   8
Practice Approach   10
Conclusion   19

**Adult Children and Their Parents: Irredeemable
Obligation and Irreplaceable Loss**   21
Harry J. Berman, PhD

Children and Parents: The Loss of Freedom   23
Children: The Irredeemable Obligation   24

Parents: The Irreplaceable Loss   27
Parents Versus Children: Exchange and Power
    Relationships   29
Conclusion: Toward Being a Good Enough Child   31

Older Adult Caregivers of Developmentally Disabled
Household Members: Service Needs and Fulfillment   **35**
        Michael S. Caserta, MS
        J. Richard Connelly, PhD
        Dale A. Lund, PhD
        James L. Poulton, MS

Method   38
Results   40
Discussion   45

Intervention With Families of the Elderly Chronically Ill:
An Alternate Approach   **51**
        Margaret R. Rodway
        Joyce Elliott
        Russel J. Sawa

Introduction   51
Family Workshop Description   54
Conclusions and Recommendations   58

The Family and Dependency: Factors Associated With
Institutional Decision-Making   **61**
        Judith G. Gonyea, PhD

Purpose of the Study   62
Methods   63
Measures   64
Limitations of the Study   69
Results   69
Implications of Findings   73

The Capacity to Care: A Family Focused Approach to
Social Work Practice With the Disabled Elderly   **79**
        Stephen T. Moore, MSW, MPA

Introduction   79
Family Provision of Care   81

Implications for Practice   85
Case Study #1   89
Case Study #2   92
Summary   93
Conclusion   94

**Burden, Coping and Health Status: A Comparison of
Family Caregivers to Community Dwelling and
Institutionalized Alzheimer's Patients**   99
         Clara Pratt, PhD
         Scott Wright, EdM
         Vicki Schmall, PhD

Method   100
Findings   103
Discussion   107

**Factors Associated With the Configuration of the Helping
Networks of Noninstitutionalized Elders**   113
         Raymond T. Coward, PhD

Methods   116
Results   119
Discussion   125
Summary   130

**Racial Differences in Family Burden: Clinical
Implications for Social Work**   133
         Richard K. Morycz, PhD, ACSW
         Julie Malloy, ACSW
         Maryann Bozich, MSW
         Pamela Martz, BA

I. Introduction and Review of Problem   133
II. Possible Clinical Implications for Practice   143
III. Conclusions   152

WORLD OF PRACTICE

Mother's Coming Home Today   155
         Frances D. Thurston, MSW

Discussion   160
Conclusion   164

Groups With Families of Elderly Long-Term Care
Residents: Building Social Support Networks   167
    Ellie Brubaker, PhD, ACSW
    Ann Ward Schiefer

The Setting   168
Development of the Group   169
Group Format   170
Outcomes of the Group   171
Summary and Conclusions   174

Assessing Caregiver Information Needs: A Brief
Questionnaire   177
    Linda J. Simonton, MSW

BOOK REVIEWS

Your Parent's Keeper: A Handbook of Psychiatric Care
for the Elderly, by J.D. Lieff   181
    Reviewed by Robert A. Famighetti, MA

Facing Death: Patients, Families, and Professionals, by
A. Stedeford   183
    Reviewed by Susan D. Henry, LCSW

Gerontological Social Work With Families
A Guide to Practice Issues and Service Delivery

FROM THE EDITOR

This special issue on *Gerontological Social Work With Families: A Guide to Practice Issues and Service Delivery* is not the result of a decision to publish such an issue, followed by a call for papers to be included in it. Instead the decision was made as we reviewed articles which had been accepted for forthcoming issues, and realized that we had a concentration of papers about the family relationships of older people, the caregiving function, and service organization and social work practice consideration in work with older families.

A review of past issues of the *Journal* testifies to the ongoing and general interest in the family among our authors. That this should be the case is understandable, because of the historical commitment of our profession to work with family groups, because of the centrality of family relationships in the lives of most older Americans, and because the task assignments of social workers in the field of aging characteristically includes work with the family of our clients.

If, as we hope, this attention to older families in the *Journal* is both reflective of and responsive to the interests and concerns of our readers, then this is a measure of progress in the field of aging and the profession of social work. It has only been in the last few decades that there has been recognition that older people are members of kinship groups, even though they do not live in multi-generation households. And even more recent is the accreditation of family members as the primary caregivers for the very old, the sick, the functionally disabled. The intellectual debts of the authors of the papers included in this issue are clear from a reading of their bibliographies, yet an iteration of these debts seems not inappropriate

1

here. Surely one of the most influential collections of papers about the family relationships of older people was that edited by Ethel Shanas and Gordon Streib. *Social Structure and the Family: Generational Relations* was published in 1965: the chapters in it were originally presented at a 2963 Symposium sponsored jointly by the Gerontological Society and Duke University, and the authors included, in addition to Shanas and Streib, Sussman, Blenkner, Rosow, Litwak, Townsend, *inter alia.* I suspect if one were to rank the influence of writings in the field and use as the measure the number of times they are cited on bibliographies, the Shanas and Streib volume would rank very high. All of these authors continued their work in this area, and they were joined by others; the importance of the works of Elaine Brody, Marjorie Cantor, Lillian Troll, Amy Horowitz, Barbara Silverstone, and others cannot be overestimated.

Despite the work of these and other scholars, Shanas in her 1979 Donald P. Kent Memorial Lecture characterized the myth of the abandonment of the old by their children as a "hydra-headed monster" which could not be killed. By which she meant that despite the array of empirical evidence to the contrary, people, including professionals in the field, continue to believe that this generation of adult children in the United States is different from all previous generations and different also from adult children in Japan, China, India and other countries. In other times, and other societies, the argument goes, the old are revered and beloved members of inter-generational households, but here and now in the United States they are the hapless victims in a culture of narcissism and their plight is one more piece of evidence of the decline of the American family. Indeed, there are those, including social workers, who argue that the availability of income maintenance, home health care, nursing homes and other services has contributed to what they see as a pervasive corruption of the sense of filial responsibility which characterized inter-generational relationships in earlier periods of American history.

It seemed to me when I listened to Shanas' lecture that her characterization of the myth was an apt one in 1979, and that although progress has been made in the years since, the myth of abandonment continues to have power. This volume, I have said, can be seen as a measure of how far we have come. *Au fond,* the authors of the papers included in this volume accept as "givens" the centrality of family relationships to the older people with whom they work. They know how important spouses and children and other relatives are to older people, and they know that family members remain the most important givers of care to older people. Not unexpectedly the focus of the papers is on functionally dependent older people, for these are the people whose need for organized social health services is most pressing, and it is the families of the chronically ill, disabled, and/or mentally impaired older people who experience most painfully the stresses which, to paraphrase Elaine Brody, must be seen as normative, expected contingencies in the careers of older people and their families.

But if this collection is a marker of progress, a careful reading of the papers gives also an indication of work yet to be done. We need, I believe, more reports from practitioners in which they write reflectively about their clinical experiences with older families. We need to know much more about older couples, the ties that bind them, the stresses which too often blight their last years together. We need to know more about what intervention strategies work, and why they work. And as always in our profession, we need work which links, as the writings of the people I cited earlier do, research findings to the world in which social workers, older people, and their families encounter each other. And finally, I believe, we need to know more about idiosyncratic, as distinguished from normative, stresses on older families. The Caserta et al. article is an example: the authors write about older adult caregivers of the developmentally disabled, and the situation of older families in which there is an adult developmentally disabled member is one of growing interest in the profession. Others come to mind as examples of emerging problems or newly recognized sources of stress in older families: I think of the article about elder abuse which have appeared in this and other *Journals,* and about the work of organizations and agencies serving older gays and their families as examples of family groups who need the best of what we have to offer.

So there are lines of inquiry yet to pursue, and practice issues which call for more systematic study. But we present this volume to our readers, certain that you will find articles of interest and usefulness to you, and also with the claim that the papers reflect the progress the profession has made.

Rose Dobrof
Editor

Social Work Practice With Family Systems in Admission to Homes for the Aged

Marion Bogo, MSW, AdvDipSW

ABSTRACT. Family systems theory provides a conceptual framework for social workers practicing with elders and their families. Processes and techniques developed in family therapy can be incorporated into social work practice approaches. In this way all family members can be helped to preserve functional relationships and modify dysfunctional family patterns that currently exist as seen in admissions to long-term facilities.

INTRODUCTION

Institutionalization of the elderly marks a life crisis in the lives of aged persons and their extended family systems. Understanding this life cycle event has led to the creation of social work services to assist elder persons in their transition from the community to the institution (Brody, 1977). There is a need to further develop knowledge, and strengthen practice approaches that focus on the dynamics and effects of this move on extended family systems. Family systems theory can provide a conceptual framework for assisting us in this regard. Procedures and techniques developed in family therapy can be adapted to intervention with extended family systems where elderly members face institutionalization. Social work services can be developed to preserve and enhance functional family relationships and to modify dysfunctional family patterns that block the families' ability to adapt and constructively deal with this life cycle event.

Marion Bogo is Social Work Practice Professor, Faculty of Social Work, University of Toronto, 246 Bloor Street West, Toronto, Ontario M5S 1A1.

5

The field of family therapy has reconceptualized the symptoms of the identified patient, usually the child, within the context of the transactions among family members. Progress in this field has been impressive in the last two decades. Theory building has led to the development of many practice models and a great variety of techniques. A growing body of research attests to the usefulness of viewing an individual's problems within the context of the family (Gurman and Kniskern, 1981). This paper shall use a family systems perspective in conceptualizing extended families as elders face institutionalization. Practice approaches useful to help families through this life cycle event will be articulated.

FAMILY INVOLVEMENT WITH THE ELDER

Aging persons as part of families has been a common theme in the social work literature in the past two decades (Leach, 1964; Millay, 1968; Miller, 1981; Tuzil, 1978; Wasser, 1966). Involvement of aging persons with their modified extended family (children, siblings, cousins) has been documented in a survey of non-institutionalized individuals 65 years of age and over (Shanas, 1979). Shanas's work, as well as that of other writers has led to a challenge of the myth that families are not involved with their elders and neglect them. Shanas (1979) has found evidence that families behave responsibly to their other members' needs, regularly perform household tasks for their older relatives and often house their relatives with them in time of crisis. Townsend (1965) found that over 45% of the older persons sampled had moved in with family until severe circumstances forced their institutionalization. York and Calysen (1977) found that families do not separate themselves from their older relatives. They found a large proportion of families in their sample helped their older relatives on many tasks, 30% took the older relatives into their home before placement, and nearly all of the families maintained frequent contact.

When families can no longer provide enough help to their elders and must seek institutionalization, involvement still predominates. York and Calsyn (1977) found that families needed assistance in making decisions regarding the placement of their relatives in an institution. After placement families maintained patterns of involvement despite physical or mental deterioration. However, the quality and enjoyment of visits were identified as problematic issues for the families. Eighty-three percent of the families indicated they would want to take part in some sort of program that might be offered by the home for their benefit including staff meetings, classes on aging, advice on how to make visits more enjoyable, and mutual aid groups with other families of residents. Thus one can conclude that most families are involved with and concerned about their elder members. At crisis points, such as when a deteriorating physical, social, or emotional situation leads to the consideration of institutionalization extended families need social work help.

FAMILY THERAPY AND GERONTOLOGY

Brody and Spark (1966) pointed out the contributions that insights from the field of family therapy could make to the crisis of institutionalization. They note that "the aged person may be symptomatic of pervasive problems in family relationships. It is therefore valid to view the family, rather than the aged person as the 'client' " (Brody & Spark, 1966, p. 78–9). The concern should be not only with the "primary client" but with the family as a whole and each of its members. Despite this recognition of the relationship between these two bodies of knowledge—family therapy and gerontology—there has been little evidence in the literature that this challenge has been responded to by those working with the aged. Bach (1980) reviewed family practice journals from 1968–78 and found three of the major journals gave attention to topics on aging in only nine issues. There has also been a lack of interest in involving the elderly in the family treatment of the child, marital distress, and current psychological and interpersonal difficulties of the adult. Notable exceptions to this trend are the works of Framo (1976), and the intergenerational family therapists Bowen (1978), and Nagy and Spark (1973). Spark (1974) points out that this area is a clinical frontier with potential for growth and change not only for the younger members of the family but for the elder as well.

FAMILY SYSTEMS THEORY

Family systems theory (Watzlawick et al., 1967) elaborates the reciprocal influence family members have on each other. Repetitive transactional patterns take on an organizing function serving to regulate the behaviour of family members as families attempt to cope with the demands of living and maintain themselves as functioning units in a state of equilibrium. These patterns or rules can be deduced as family members communicate and interact.

Family therapists have developed a variety of dimensions to understand better the transactional dynamics of a particular family. In social work practice with elders and their families the following concepts have proven to be useful; structural dimensions of boundaries, alignments, and power (Minuchin, 1974); communication patterns that describe content and relationship levels, verbal and non-verbal messages, openness and receptivity (Walzlawick, 1967).

"The boundaries of a subsystem are the rules defining who participates and how" (Minuchin, 1974, p. 53). These rules dictate who is included and who is excluded in an event, and define the roles of those included in relation to each other and to the outside world.

Minuchin (1974) conceives all families as falling somewhere along a continuum of very diffuse boundaries (the "enmeshed" family) and over-rigid boundaries (the "disengaged" family). The enmeshed family is characterized by members who are over-joined, over-reactive, and over-responsive. The mutual over-involvement is such that change in any one family member reverberates throughout the entire family. For example, in Homes for the Elderly one can observe the family who becomes very distraught in relation to their elder's complaint about the food served. Various members of the family will call the home and discuss concerns with staff. Messages will be relayed throughout the family.

Disengaged family members tend to be disconnected and isolated with little dependence on each other for their functioning. Little interest is shown, communication and co-operative effort is difficult. For example, in such families there is usually little interest in or knowledge of the visiting patterns of other family members. As a result the senior may rarely see family members or have them all appear around a holiday or birthday.

Alignment refers to the "joining or opposition of one member of a system to another in carrying out an operation" (Aponte & Van Deusen, 1981, p. 313). Within the boundaries of any family the members have patterns of working together or in mutual opposition in relation to the many activities they must engage in as family members.

Power has been defined as

> the relative influence of each (family) member on the outcome of the activity. . . . Power is generated by the way family members actively and passively combine, enabling the intention of one or more of the members to prevail in determining the outcome of a transaction. (Aponte & Van Deusen, 1981, p. 313)

As the aging person begins to lose control over some of their biological processes they may be in need of more care. In this situation they may inadvertently discover that their weakening condition has given them more power over the frequency of visits from their significant family members, the amount of care and attention given to them, and the degree of involvement of their children with them. A somewhat disengaged family member may be influenced to become more involved as a result of the deterioration of the elder.

Communication refers to listening, understanding the other, and expressing oneself clearly and accurately. Communication concerns itself with the content and process of the family's verbal and non-verbal information sending and receiving (Watzlawick et al., 1967). Does the family talk to each other about the present situation? How open are they in expressing thoughts and feelings? How frequently do they speak? Who is dominant? Do the family members listen to each other or do they interrupt? Do the members respond to verbal and non-verbal messages? Do the members think they are being heard and understood?

In situations relating to admission to a Home for the Aged, the content of the communication often relates to poor prognosis, deteriorating conditions, feelings of sadness and loss. As this material is painful families tend to avoid speaking directly about the issues, or offer false reassurance to the elder. In addition, family members tend to leave the elder person out of the preliminary discussions about future plans for fear of upsetting the elder or believing he/she will not understand. As a result, when a family interview is finally held one can observe many instances of incongruent communication. For example, the adult children will be talking about what is best for mother and the elder begins to slump, hangs her head lower, and is quiet. When the worker asks the elder what are her thoughts about the application she may look wistfully at the worker and say with a sigh, "I'll leave that up to my children, they seem to know what's best for me."

Physical and/or mental deterioration of elder family members begins a new phase in families' life cycles and constitutes a precipitant to unbalance the present equilibrium. Institutionalization impacts the entire family and will effect and be effected by the characteristic family transactional patterns. Social workers and other personnel working with elders and their families in relation to admission to a Home for the Aged can be assisted in their assessment, planning and intervention through use of a family systems orientation.

The following practice approach rests on such an orientation and makes use of principles and techniques developed by family therapy models. Social work students at Metropolitan Toronto Homes for the Aged were instructed and supervised in the use of this model with new applicants to three separate Homes. Staff observation of the positive effects on elders and families led to adoption of this method throughout all eight Homes for the Aged (Singer & Wells, 1981).

PRACTICE APPROACH

The primary goal of the social worker in this practice approach is to help the entire family deal most effectively with the situational needs brought on by aging. Helping families develop and implement a workable and satisfactory plan is the goal for intervention.

Engagement

As soon as a request for admission to a Home is received, the social worker sets an appointment for a family interview. This procedure makes explicit the belief that involvement of many significant family members facilitates the continuance and enhancement of positive intergenerational relationships. Immediate family involvement enables the social worker to define his/her role as helping the family find the best solution to the issue they are facing as a result of the situational problems brought on by aging or physical illness. Participants in the decision-making process are more committed to a plan that they have participated in formulating. Resistance to a plan can be dealt with when it is observed and acknowledged. Where family members have a history of conflictual relationships there may be great reluctance to attend together. The worker needs to reassure the family that the focus will not be on past difficulties. The focus will be on dealing constructively with the present situation, with structure and direction in the meeting given by the worker.

At the first meeting the worker states the purpose as helping the family to develop and implement the best possible plan for that family and the elder to meet the bio-psycho-social needs engendered by illness or aging. The tasks of this phase are to join with the family so that together an assessment of the actual bio-psycho-social needs of the elder can be made to establish to what extent the family group has made use of community-based alternatives. Attention should be paid to the extent to which family factors facilitate or interfere with the use of such resources. As well, the elder's readiness or reluctance to use these services should be considered.

The worker will need to join with each family member and the elder in order to gain an understanding of their perception of the problem. This should be done systematically so that all members have an opportunity to express their thoughts and feelings directly, and to see where there is similarity and difference within the family. The worker should use time flexibly and establish a longer interview session for a larger family. As the family may consist of many members, inexperienced workers may prefer a co-worker or supervisor present with them in the initial session.

Assessment

The focus should be on the present, on learning about the current situation, and how the family is coping, both functionally and emotionally. As well, the worker should be assessing the nature of the family dynamics in relation to boundaries between the units, alignments, power, and communication patterns.

Assessment should focus on: (1) clarifying the meaning of the request for admission and the reality of the presenting situation. It is necessary to establish the time frame regarding the problem, that is, is this a chronic or acute situation and why is this a problem now; what are the expectations of the various family members regarding institutionalization; how realistic are these expectations; what needs would be met, and what would be unmet through admission; (2) clarifying whether there are major changes taking place in the family system which cannot be dealt with usefully by admission. A frequent example of this is the death of one spouse leading to normal grief and mourning by the other. Family members stressed by their perception of their parent's suffering may prematurely precipitate a request for admission to a home. Accompanying normal mourning the elder may experience temporary impaired functioning. Extra family or community-based supports may be sufficient to assist the elder to remain in their own home through this difficult phase. Rather than accepting the normality of the grief and its associated affects and behaviours, families may try to "do something" to lessen their parent's sadness. If re-location is the attempted solution, it may further exacerbate the situation and turn a normal life stage process into a problem situation; (3) clarifying the position in the family system of the person initiating the request. Who has decided that something has to be done and why? Is that person acting as the family spokesperson or expressing their own thoughts and concerns?

As the discussion of these issues proceeds family dynamics quickly become apparent. Old unresolved family issues and relationship problems will be re-awakened and may be intensified as they are re-enacted in relation to a new problem. In those families who have avoided dealing with unresolved issues both the style of avoidance and the past issues themselves may serve as a deterrent to current effective family problem solving. The worker will have the opportunity to observe and experience the communication style, power positions, boundaries, and alliances which exist within the family. These data form the basis for a family systems assessment as discussed earlier. Such an assessment leads the worker to identify the extent to which particular family dynamics will be facilitative or resistive in the development of a realistic plan to meet the needs of the elder. Where family dynamics are facilitative of effective problem solving the worker can join with those forces and reinforce family capacity. Where family dynamics become obstacles to effective family problem solving the worker will need to intervene to change these processes, using the techniques of family therapy.

Case Example

For example, Mr. Jones, a 78-year-old man requested admission to the Home. Mr. Jones, married for 50 years, had been widowed two years ago. He had two daughters, aged 45 and 40, both married, living in the same city, with children. He had two siblings, a younger sister of 70 maintaining herself in the community, and a younger brother of 74, retired and living in the country. Since the death of his wife, Mr. Jones had been actively grieving, felt sad, and somewhat hopeless, tended to be reclusive, and generally not able to make a positive social readjustment to his new status as widower. He had tended to regularly visit his older daughter who early in the interviews revealed herself as the decision maker in the family now that her mother had died. This daughter (Jane) had taken on many care-taking functions for Mr. Jones, shopping for him, preparing meals, organizing his schedule. In the past three months Jane had completed a course as a real estate saleswoman and wanted to pursue this career. She was no longer able to provide as much care-giving activities to her father as previously, and had encouraged him to move into the Home. When she informed her sister, Sally, of "Dad's decision" Sally accepted this, as the family rule was "Jane knows best." In the extended family interview it became apparent that there were many resources in Mr. Jones' family and community networks which were capable of providing physical, social and emotional supports such as Sally, Mr. Jones' sister, the Church, the Community Meals-on-Wheels and so on. However, the system dynamic in this family was that Jane was perceived as (and in fact was) a highly competent, efficient, and controlling woman who did many things well. The entire family perceived Sally as less capable and less powerful than Jane. Both sons-in-law also deferred to Jane. As Jane's aunt commented caustically, "She is very capable, and if you forget that she'll be quick to remind you." Thus, Mr. Jones was prematurely moving to institutionalization as the result of a family myth that "Jane knows best" and a family rule that "no one challenges Jane's authority."

In order for the extended family group to clarify the nature of Mr. Jones' needs and the alternative solutions available to them two family patterns needed to be modified. The first pattern was Jane's power position in the family hierarchy. This position excluded others from participating in problem solving and left Jane feeling overburdened and resentful. Jane needed to relinquish this position of power in the family and move into an equalitarian position so that her father, his siblings, and her sister could participate more fully in the process of determining Mr. Jones' needs and planning for effective ways of meeting them. Secondly, the communication patterns in the family reflected the structure of family relationships. Jane tended to dominate the family sessions, giving directives to other family members. She would ask for other members' opinions. They would hesitantly offer a guarded opinion. However, Jane then tended to discount or not listen to what was said. The family member would then withdraw, leaving Jane in an unchallenged position.

The worker joined with this extended family group in relation to the presenting request for admission to the home. She demonstrated respect for the family system by initially relating to each person, facilitating their expression of concerns and opinions, and reflecting and clarifying those concerns. She attempted to raise the family's comfort level through demonstrating acceptance and empathy regarding their perception of the situation. As the interview progressed, the family dynamics became apparent. The communication style of the family led the worker to form hypotheses about the family structure. She inquired about roles and decision making processes in the family and developed the formulation of family dynamics as described above.

Family intervention first focused on helping the family to modify the communication patterns that were operating to keep Jane in a dominant position. The worker encouraged each person to speak for themselves. She structured open and direct communication and responses between various members of the family. She blocked Jane's over-responsiveness and encouraged under-responsive members to verbalize their thoughts and feelings. She clarified the importance and expectation of direct communication in relation to the matters under discussion. In this manner, the worker began to engage the entire family in exploring the issues confronting Mr. Jones and the possibilities of his remaining in the community. As the worker helped modify Jane's dominant position in the family structure, Sally and Mr. Jones' sister began to take a more active role in the family interviews. The worker encouraged Mr. Jones to re-assert his position in the family as well. After four such interviews were held a more active and animated family group began to emerge capable of effective problem-solving on behalf of the elder in the family.

Pre-Admission

Many families are able to move with the elder from the stage of a mutual and shared assessment to a sound plan to remain in the community using additional resources. Other families move through the process of assessment to a plan for admission to a care facility. For this group of families involvement in preparation for admission is a helpful method for continuing involvement with the elder and responding to the needs of the extended family group in a time of transition. A program for families and the elder where they can gain knowledge necessary to help them deal with the institution which will now be a significant unit in their system is useful. The family needs to learn how to remain meaningfully involved with their elder. As well, the family needs to learn how to be an active, involved advocate for the elder with the institution staff. To function in this way the family needs knowledge of the medical condition of the elder, its expected progress and response to medical treatment. The family also needs knowledge of the institution, its routines and rules, policies about visitors and the elder leaving for visits. The family needs to meet significant personnel and learn their respective roles and styles. A variety of methods can be used to transmit this knowledge. Meetings of groups of relatives, using lecture, discussion, slides, films, and written material are effective. In addition, each family should meet with members of the interdisciplinary team who will be assigned to care for their elder member. This meeting serves the purpose of relationship building, information exchange, and clarification of roles and responsibilities of family members and of the staff.

Admission

The social worker needs to be particularly active as admission to the facility takes place. In this phase, the reality of the transition from community to Home has its major impact. All family members may re-experience any ambivalence that was felt in the earlier stage. Issues that appeared to have been resolved may re-surface needing to be re-worked. The worker should hold regular family interviews at this point and help family members express clearly and directly their thoughts and feelings regarding the move. The worker should label mixed feelings as normal, should link current concerns to family dynamics observed or discussed, should review for the family the work they have done together, and should offer concrete suggestions where appropriate.

It has been observed that where family members do not have the opportunity to work out their thoughts and feelings in relation to the admission, there is a greater likelihood that these unresolved issues will be acted out through avoidance of the elder and the Home, or overly critical and demanding stances in relation to the nursing staff and the care given. In helping families deal more directly with their feelings and concerns about admission to the home it is expected that a difficult transition from community to institutional living can be accomplished while maintaining and strengthening the ties of the elder and his extended family.

Case Example

Mrs. Black, daughter of Mr. Gold, a 74-year-old man requested admission of her father to the Home. Mr. Gold, married for 44 years, had been widowed 2-1/2 years ago. He had
two married children, Mr. Gold, Jr., 36, and Mrs. Black,
33, living and working in the same city, with children. His
siblings lived a great distance away in another city. He presented as a socially isolated man. Mr. Gold had suffered two
heart attacks, and was prone to angina. He was anxious and
fearful about another heart attack and dying alone. He was
frail and forgetful, increasingly unable to care for himself.
Recently he had been telephoning his daughter up to five
times a day with these concerns. Medical and psychiatric con-
sultants advised that his medical condition was precarious and
that he should not be living alone. Feeling depressed and
frightened he was indirectly asking his daughter to care for
him. She had explored many community resources and had
concluded that since she would not have him live with her, he
needed institutionalization.

Through a number of family interviews the following assessment emerged. Mrs. Gold had been a lively, dominant,
powerful leader in this family. She had bound her nuclear
family to her and they were a highly enmeshed group. Her
son had, in early adulthood, attempted to gain some distance
from the family through withdrawal, avoidance, and silence.
These behaviours were met with active, but unsuccessful,
pressure on his mother's part to reinvolve him. Mrs. Gold had
died of cancer 2-1/2 years ago after a six-month illness. Her
loss as the central force in the family left a leadership vacuum
which her daughter quickly assumed. Her father attempted to
transfer his reliance and involvement from his wife to his
daughter. She had found this situation increasingly burdensome and had turned to her brother. In this respect she took
on her mother's struggle with her brother to engage him in a
closer family relationship. As with his mother before, her
brother responded to her efforts by withdrawal, avoidance,
and silence. She responded to this with angry, critical attacks.
Mr. Gold, Sr. remained passive and depressed as he observed
his children battling with each other.

In order for this family to develop a plan to meet the physical, emotional, and social needs of their elder, family patterns needed to be modified. Some resolution of the enmeshment/disengagement issue with acceptance of the roles and behaviours associated with these positions needed to occur. Additionally, the communication sequence of attack-retreat-attack needed to change.

The worker joined with this family group by initially relating to each person, clarifying their concerns about the presenting situation. Recognizing Mrs. Black's over-involvement in the system relative to her brother, the worker aligned with Mr. Gold, Jr. and encouraged him to express his thoughts and feelings. The worker actively blocked Mrs. Black's attempts to attack her brother and continue their on-going struggle. The worker did make the struggle explicit, reframing the content. "Both (Mrs. Black and Mr. Gold, Jr.) of you feel alone, misunderstood, and disappointed with each other." This definition of the problem allowed the siblings to engage with the worker in dealing with their relationship. Beginning with the presenting situation of planning for their father's care, they could clarify how different their expectations were, relate this to their parents' perceptions and positions as they were growing up, and over time begin to move to some compromise regarding the degree and nature of their involvement.

Mr. Gold, Sr. was present throughout these sessions and the worker attempted to involve him in the decisions and reflections about the family. Both he and his children did not want to change his long-standing position in the family as "someone to be taken care of." Therefore, the family work consisted mainly of helping the siblings sort out their relationship and communication so that they were able to arrive at a joint decision regarding care, and specific roles and responsibilities regarding the move into the Home and ongoing involvement with their father.

During the transition period, when Mr. Gold moved into the Home and began to settle in, the worker continued to see the family regularly, further clarifying agreements and understandings that had been made, reinforcing Mr. Gold, Jr.'s involvement, tempering Mrs. Black's tendency to attack when her brother was disappointing her, and holding the two siblings to examination and resolution of issues in their relationship. Through family systems intervention long-standing dysfunctional patterns were modified and increased positive involvement was achieved between Mr. Gold and his children both during and after the move into the Home.

CONCLUSION

Involvement of the extended family system in the transition from community to institutional living is of concern to social workers working with the aged. Contributions from family systems and family therapy offer knowledge and techniques which can enrich the variety of programs and approaches used to service this growing population group.

BIBLIOGRAPHY

Aponte, H.J. and Van Deusen, J.M. "Structural Family Therapy." In A.S. Gurman and D.P. Kniskern (Eds.), *Handbook of Family Therapy*. New York: Brunner/Mazel, Inc., 1981.

Bach, F. "Family Therapy Excludes the Elderly." In D.S. Freeman (Ed.), *Perspectives on Family Therapy*. Canada: Butterworth & Co., 1980.

Bowen, M. *Family Therapy in Clinical Practice*. New York: Jason Aronson, 1978.

Brody, E.M. and Spark, G.M. "Institutionalization of the Aged: A Family Crisis." *Family Process*, 1966, 5(1), 76–90.

Brody, E.M. *Long Term Care of Older People*. New York: Human Sciences Press, 1977.

Framo, J. "Family of Origin as a Therapeutic Resource for Adults in Marital and Family Therapy." *Family Process*, 1976, 15(1), 193–210.

Gurman, A.S. and D.P. Kniskern (Eds.), *Handbook of Family Therapy*. New York: Brunner/Mazel, Inc., 1981.

Leach, J.M. "The Intergenerational Approach in Casework with the Aging." *Social Casework*, 1964, 45(3), 144–149.

Millay, M. "Casework with the Older Person and His Family." In F.J. Turner (Ed.), *Differential Diagnosis & Treatment in Social Work*. New York: The Free Press, 1968.

Miller, D.A. "The 'Sandwich' Generation: Adult Children of the Aging." *Social Work*, 1981, 26(5), 419–423.

Minuchin, S. *Families and Family Therapy*. Cambridge, Mass: Harvard University Press, 1974.

Nagy, I.B. and Spark, G. *Invisible Loyalties*. New York: Harper and Row, 1973.

Shanas, E. "The Family as a Social Support System in Old Age." *Gerontologist*, 1979, 19(2), 169–175.

Singer, C.B. and Wells, L.M. "The Impact of Student Units on Services and Structural Change in Homes for the Aged." *Canadian Journal of Social Work Education*, 1981, 8(3), 11–27.

Spark, G.M. "Grandparents and Intergenerational Family Therapy." *Family Process*, 1974, 13(2), 225–237.

Townsend, P. "The Effects of Family Structure on the Likelihood of Admission to an Institution in Old Age: The Application of a General Theory." In E. Shanas and G.F. Streib (Eds.), *Social Structure and the Family*. New Jersey: Prentice-Hall, Inc., 1965.

Tuzil, T. "The Agency Role in Helping Middle-Aged Children and Their Parents." *Social Casework*, 1978, 59(5), 302–305.

Wasser, E. "Family Casework Focus on the Older Person." *Social Casework*, 1966, 47(7), 423–431.

Watzlawick, P., Beavin, J., and Jackson, J. *Pragmatics of Human Communication*. New York: W.W. Norton & Company, 1967.

York, L. and Calsyn, R.J. "Family Involvement in Nursing Homes." *Gerontologist*, 1977, 17, 500–505.

Adult Children and Their Parents: Irredeemable Obligation and Irreplaceable Loss

Harry J. Berman, PhD

ABSTRACT. Although the strong preference among older people is for independent living, a variety of problems can lead parents to move in with adult children. This living arrangement entails distinct social-psychological characteristics. By drawing on theoretical constructs from sociology and social psychology this paper explores these characteristics in terms of feelings related to the loss of freedom, the children's sense of irredeemable obligation and the parents' sense of irreplaceable loss. Based on this analysis, recommendations are made regarding attitudinal changes which can increase both parents' and children's degree of satisfaction with this living arrangement.

Despite our cultural love affair with the extended family—where parents, grandparents, children and assorted dogs, cats and other livestock live under one roof (Bane, 1976), generally neither parents nor adult children want to live in the same household. The strong preference, particularly among aging parents, has consistently been found to be for parents, even widowed parents, and adult children to maintain separate households (Laslett, 1976; Lopata, 1973; Troll, 1970).

Those preferences are reflected in the actual living arrangements of older people in our society. Approximately 80 percent of all older people in our society have living children (Atchley and Miller, 1980; Bengtson and Treas, 1980; Cicirelli, 1983). However the proportion of older people who share a household with those children is considerably smaller. Based on a national probability sample, Shanas (1979) estimates that

Dr. Berman is Associate Professor, Child, Family and Community Services Program, Sangamon State University, Springfield, IL 62708.

21

18% of all people over 65 who have living children share households with one or more of them. (This figure includes parents who live in the children's homes and children who live in the parents' homes.) Moreover, the trend has been away from multigenerational sharing of households and toward generational household separation. One indicator of this trend is the proportion of older men and women who live in households as an "other relative." The term "other relative" is used by the Census Bureau to designate a kin member who is neither the head of the household nor the wife of the head of the household and who is living in the household. In recent years there has been a steady decline in the numbers of elderly who live in households with their children or other kin. In 1940, 15% of older men lived with their kin as "other relatives." In 1975 only about 4% did. For women there has also been a decline in living with kin, though not to the same extent as for men. In 1940, 30% of older women lived with kin; in 1975, only 13% did (Mindel, 1979).

But people do not always get to live their lives—much less their entire lives—according to their preferences. As life expectancy increases, the proportion of people living to ages beyond 75, ages characterized by declining health and capacities (Neugarten, 1975), also increases. Most of the research on living arrangements is cross-sectional. Accurate estimates of the probability of an aging parent moving in with adult children at some point in the family life cycle will wait long-term longitudinal studies. However, one recent short-term longitudinal study can be used to provide an initial estimate of the frequency of this event for contemporary families. Fillenbaum and Wallman (1984) tracked the living arrangements of a random sample of 276 older community residents over a 30-month period. At the first time of measurement 25% of the sample was categorized as living with kin, but without a spouse. At the end of two and one-half years an additional 8% of the sample had shifted into this category (7% had shifted out of it). Thus it seems reasonable to conclude that it is not unusual for adult children to be confronted with the issue of making a place in their homes for aging parents and for the parents to be confronted with the issue of adjusting to such an arrangement.

Moving in with an adult child is more likely to occur to

older women than to older men and to the old-old (75+) rather than to the young-old (Mindel, 1979). Also, lower income levels and higher levels of incapacity increase the likelihood of parents moving in with adult children (Fengler, Danigelis and Little, 1983). Among older parents who live with an adult child, 65% live with a daughter, compared with 35% who live with a son (Hendricks and Hendricks, 1981).

This living arrangement entails several distinct social-psychological characteristics. These characteristics can be thought of as stresses which are potentially present in all cases where a parent has moved in with an adult child, regardless of the particular health, social, or economic problem which precipitated the move.

CHILDREN AND PARENTS: THE LOSS OF FREEDOM

The first factor that should be recognized is implicit in what has already been cited regarding preferred living arrangements. Generally, both the adult children and the parents would prefer some other living arrangement. Therefore, when a parent moves in with an adult child, it is not usually because either party really wants it that way. Phrases like "if all other things were equal" or "if the neighborhood hadn't changed" or "if my son hadn't moved away" reflect the feelings that go along with reluctance to make this decision. Naturally, both parents and children could choose not to make the decision for the parent to live with the adult child. But one should not be misled by the use of the word "choice" here. Experientially this is not a free choice situation, but rather a situation in which people are compelled to do something to avoid a less desirable alternative. Although many events occur in life where people are forced to endure outcomes they wouldn't voluntarily choose, people tend to believe and act as if they can control and master their own fate (Wicklund, 1974; Lefcourt, 1973; Deci, 1980). The loss of behavioral freedom is associated with a variety of negative consequences including impaired performance in learning situations (Perlmutter and Monty, 1977); reduced ability to respond adaptively in stressful situations (Janis and Leventhal, 1968); antisocial behaviors (Zimbardo, 1969); and physical disease (Schmale, 1971). Loss of freedom can also result in feelings of hostility (Worchel, 1974), though such negative feelings may be repressed (Deci, 1980).

In the case of parents coming to live with adult children it is reasonable to assume the presence of hostile feelings associated with being compelled to accept a non-preferred living arrangement, but also to recognize that these feelings may be repressed by both parties. Long periods of time may elapse where neither children nor parents express the hostility regarding loss of control over their fate, but the living arrangement's origin as something people were forced into means that the potential for the expression of such feelings persists. Furthermore, even if the child or the parent succeeded in blocking the expression of feelings of hostility, the other member of the relationship might not. And once such feelings surface in an interaction, they perpetuate themselves. If I resent living with you and you become aware of my resentment, soon you will resent my feeling of resentment. The very feeling one or the other person was trying to block or repress then breaks out like a kind of epidemic and takes over the relationship for a period of time. If parents and children are lucky, the outbreak may be shortlived. If not so lucky, the disease may persist. But even if a return of hostile feelings to a repressed level is achieved, it is worth recognizing that the causes of these feelings, which derive from the loss of control over one's life, have not been removed.

An important point to recognize here is that people generally tend to look at this situation from the children's point of view: their hostility over being forced to take in parents. But the parents also experienced what was a non-preferred choice, a forced move, and also are likely to harbor feelings of hostility over being forced to do something they did not really want to do, feelings which they, too, are trying to control.

CHILDREN: THE IRREDEEMABLE OBLIGATION

In what sense are children forced to make the decision to have a parent come live with them? There is no law requiring children to do this. Nor are children forced to accept their parents through any form of physical coercion. Rather the force here derives from a socially recognized norm: one's duty to one's parents. Besides the historical roots of the idea of duty to one's parents in the Judeo-Christian tradition, this norm is also linked to the norm of reciprocity (Gouldner, 1960). When others perform services for us, especially voluntary and unsolicited services, we experience gratitude and want to reciprocate when the giver needs our help. The norm of reciprocity is especially strong in filial relationships. Children are indebted to their parents for the care they received when young and for the "ultimate gift" of life itself.

The norm of reciprocity is especially interesting because of the imbalance between the initial giver and the receiver, an imbalance which persists even after the gift has been reciprocated. The sociologist Georg Simmel has written.

> . . . [o]nce we have received something good from another person, once he has preceded us with his action, we no longer can make up for it completely, no matter how much our own return gift or service may objectively or legally surpass his own. The reason is that his gift, because it was the first, has a voluntary character which no return gift can have. For, to return the benefit we are obliged ethically; we operate under a coercion which though neither social nor legal but moral, is still a coercion. The first gift is given in full spontaneity; it has a freedom without any duty. . . . Only when we give first are we free, and this is the reason why, in the first gift, which is not occasioned by any gratitude, there lies a beauty, a spontaneous devotion to the other, an opening up and flowering from the "virgin soil" of the soul, as it were, which *cannot be matched* by any subsequent gift, no matter how superior in content. (Blau, 1981)

Simmel's example is written in terms of the general relations between people in society. In the case of parents and children, where the initial gift is that of life and nurturance, the imbalance created by being the initial recipient, the inability to reciprocate fully, is even more pronounced. As Zena Blau (1981) has put it, children have an irredeemable obligation toward parents. Nothing they do can ever make up for the initial parental gift. It is reasonable to assume, therefore, that one factor which leads to the decision of an adult child to care for parent in his or her home is the socially recognized and personally felt obligation to pay back one's parents for the early care received from them. Further, because of the way the norm of reciprocity works, because of the nature of gift giving and receiving, and because of the magnitude of the gift received from the parent, this obligation can never be paid back in full. It is irredeemable as long as the parent lives: you can never fully pay back your parents for what they gave you. Taking a parent into your home doesn't fully pay them back. Cooking for them doesn't do it. Cutting back on your social life doesn't do it. Even bathing them and changing bedpans doesn't do it. Obviously a situation in which one can never do enough is a situation tailor-made for feelings of guilt and frustration.

The potential for guilt and frustration is made even greater because of another feature of the children's lives: The adult children of aging parents are likely themselves to be parents. If their children are small, there will be a pull in terms of the time and energy required by the small children. However, even if the children of the sons and daughters in the middle generation are grown, the tendency is for those middle generation parents to be quite involved in the lives of their children. For example, Lowenthal, Thurnher and Chiriboga (1975) report on the sources of stress in the lives of middle-aged and pre-retirement women. The participants in the study were asked to rate each year of their past life on a nine point scale of satisfaction/dissatisfaction. They were also asked to describe the events in the preceding ten years which led to changes in their level of satisfaction or dissatisfaction. The changes these women encountered generally related to the lives of others. Problems that *other* people experienced had led to stress in *their* lives. And the "other people" for them often were their grown children. In describing a decline in her life satisfaction, one respondent said "That was when my daughter left her husband and three children. I should rate it number one (lowest level of life satisfaction) because it nearly killed me." Another respondent said, in explaining a sharp decrease in her level of life satisfaction, "Mark, my son, got sick at school and when he is unhappy I am unhappy" (Lowenthal et al., 1975). The point is that these women are very involved emotionally with their children's lives at the same time they may be having to cope with their aging parents.

It is appropriate to focus on middle-aged women because it is far more common for aging parents to move in with daughters than with sons (Treas, 1975). Thus, the problem of this intergenerational squeeze is largely, though not entirely, the problem of middle-aged women. The way that women in middle adulthood are subject to a generational cross-fire has received attention in the professional and popular literature (Brody, 1981; Rubin, 1979). Mid-life women experience pressures to be concerned about their young adult children, their husbands' job success and health, as well as their aging parents. Troll, Miller and Atchley (1979) term this set of pressures the Cassandra Complex. In addition to their concerns about family, women in middle adulthood are becoming new members or continuing as members of the work force. The tremendous increase in the past 20 years in women's employment is commonly recognized. What is not so commonly known is that the largest increase in employment has been among women between the ages of 40 to 59 (Hendricks and Hendricks, 1981). Thus, the potential for guilt and frustration which stems from the irredeemable nature of the obligation felt by adult children toward aging parents is made even more difficult by stresses associated with other family and work obligations.

PARENTS: THE IRREPLACEABLE LOSS

If the children are faced with an irredeemable obligation, what of the aging parents? What factors lead to a parent's decision to move in with a child—a living arrangement that is not preferred by most older people? The particular circumstances vary, but the general cause is an accumulation of losses involving the capacity to care for one's self. The most prominent of such losses involve losses of health related to life-threatening diseases. However, the capacity to live independently may also be lost through health problems which are not acutely life-threatening, such as loss of vision, loss of hearing, loss of mobility, or loss of memory. Typically, there is not one loss, but multiple losses. In one study of adult children and aging parents, such multiple losses in parents were described in a very realistic, but non-technical way as "general physical decline." This term can be viewed as a label for a collection of conditions which separately could be managed by the older person living alone but together make independent life impossible (Simos, 1973).

Health losses are easily seen as factors which precipitate a move in with an adult child. Those health losses are accompanied by other losses which, though often less visible or less important to the adult children, are very significant to the aging parent. Such losses include the loss of work, the loss of a lifetime home or the right to drive an automobile, the deaths of friends or even the death of a pet. Each of these constitutes an attachment or connection of the person with the world. It is through such attachments that our identities are manifested to ourselves and to others (Levinson, 1978). The loss of a substantial number of such attachments can be experienced as the loss of a substantial portion of the self. Although younger people, through accident or illness, may also experience extensive losses, and therefore substantial alterations in their attachments with the world, the losses experienced by older people by and large can never be replaced; they are lost and gone forever, and they are irreplaceable.

The irreplaceableness of the losses of old age is related to the way that our lives are lived during a particular period of time. For example, since the legalization of gambling in Atlantic City many older people have had to move because of the condominiumizing of apartment houses. From the 1950s through the mid-1970s Atlantic City was, to a substantial degree, a retirement community for most of the year. The Boardwalk was like an outdoor multipurpose senior center with no funding problems. When the older people of Atlantic City moved away it was not only their apartments which they lost. The real loss was the loss of the community in which they had lived. Atlantic City is still there, but the community is gone. That particular community existed only during a twenty year period during the second half of the twentieth century. It can never be replaced.

The children of aging parents may think in terms of their parents replacing lost attachments and emphasize the need to get out and make new friends and develop new interests. For the parents, however, the issue may not be lack of social skills or shyness or difficulty in making new contacts, which is the way the children would describe the problem (Simos, 1973), but rather a sense of hopelessness at ever replacing people and places that existed at a particular moment in history, a moment that can never happen again. Children are often puzzled by parents who were outgoing and sociable when younger but who come to depend on them for any kind of social life (Simos, 1973). The perceived outgoingness and sociability may have had as much to do with the parent's network of acquaintances and social setting as with any underlying personality trait. It is not so much that the parent's personalities have changed as that the world in which the personalities were embedded has changed. With the disappearance of that supporting social world the trait of sociability may also disappear.

PARENTS VERSUS CHILDREN: EXCHANGE AND POWER RELATIONSHIPS

When the cause of the parent's need to live with the child is a loss of the personal resources required for independent living the parents are particularly vulnerable. This vulnerability can be appreciated by the application of exchange theory:

> The basic assumption underlying exchange theory is that interactions between individuals or between groups can be viewed as attempts to maximize rewards (both material and non-material) and reduce costs. . . . It is often the case that one of the participants in the exchange values the rewards gained in the relationship more than the other. It is in these situations that the variable of power enters into the analysis. From this perspective power is synonymous with the dependence of Actor A upon Actor B. (Dowd, 1975)

Older people in general, and older people who reside with their adult children in particular, are at a great disadvantage in terms of exchange (Bengtson and Treas, 1980). They have little to exchange, and the less they have to exchange, the more powerless they become.

Another way to characterize this situation is through an idea known as the Principle of Least Interest. This idea was developed in a study of college dating practices conducted in the 1930's by William Waller (Waller, 1938). Waller noted that the person with the least commitment to maintaining a relationship was in the best position to control the relationship because he or she had the least to lose if the relationship was broken. By contrast, the person with the greatest commitment must often make concessions to the will of the other in order to avoid the severance of the relationship (Bengtson and Treas, 1980).

The Principle of Least Interest is applicable to the situation of parents living with adult children. Parents have more at stake than children in this arrangement. The irredeemable obligation under which the children live is tempered considerably by their power over their parents, power which arises from the irreplaceable losses sustained by the parents. These losses lead to reduced resources for use in exchange for the services the parents receive.

There are two strategies which the parents can employ in this situation. The first is compliance. When there is nothing which a person has that is of value to another—not money, not approval of their actions, not esteem for them (Dowd, 1975)—then what is left is compliance. The exchange of compliance for continued care-giving by a more powerful child may be central in cases of abuse of older people.

The second strategy available to parents is guilt. When a parent "lays a guilt trip" on a child who has taken the parent into his or her home, it is as if an inflation factor has been brought into the exchange relationship. The parent is, in effect, saying that the care the child is giving is not worth much, just as inflation reduces the worth of dollars. Since, under this strategy, the care received by the parent is not worth much, the parent is not really in debt to the child and need not give back anything—even compliance—in return. This strategy only works up to a point. It is risky. It depends upon the child's willingness to assume guilt. If children stop feeling guilty, if the obligation is no longer felt as being irredeemable, then it can become painfully clear where the power in the relationship really lies.

CONCLUSION: TOWARD BEING A GOOD ENOUGH CHILD

The negative social-psychological characteristics which exist when parents come to live with adult children are not the only ones that are present. Besides these negative features there are satisfactions and benefits which are possible for both parents and children. Depending on the degree of disability, the parent may be able to assist the child in the management of the household. Living together means that the parents can witness and participate in the successes of their children and in their troubles; and the children, in turn, have someone on hand with whom they can share those successes and those troubles. Living together means that the children have a tangible way to show their love for their parents, love which may be felt very deeply.

The limited evidence available does not show high levels of dissatisfaction with this living arrangement or low levels of morale among parents who live with their children. For example Beland (1984) in a study of urban Canadian elderly, found an inverse relationship between living with a child and filing an application for a housing change or expressing a desire for such a change. Fengler, Danigelis and Little (1983) in a study of urban and rural elderly in Vermont found no significant difference in morale among older people living with others and older married couples living alone. Kivett and Learner (1982) in a study of rural, North Carolina elderly found that when effects of differences in perceived health status were controlled there was no significant difference in morale of adults living with children and those in other living arrangements.

Nonetheless, the stresses in this situation deserve attention. Ways to deal with these stresses are badly needed. Some of the ways to deal with these stresses involve groups outside the family. The availability of a service such as adult day care can make the difference between premature nursing home placement of the parent and the parent's continued ability to live with a family. But adult day care is expensive and not readily available in many places. Sometimes what is needed is just occasional help, a respite, someone to keep an eye on the parent if the children are gone.

But even with adult day care, respite cooperatives, and other services such as visiting nurses and nutrition centers, most of the responsibility for managing the stresses of this living arrangement rests with the family and depends on the *attitudes of both children and parents.*

Recognition should be given by the children to their parents' desire to maintain control over at least some area of the family's life. Symbolic exchanges can be a useful means by which the parent can maintain some degree of autonomy (Bengtson and Treas, 1980).

The parents, however, have a reciprocal obligation. They must be willing to give up old patterns of independent functioning and allow the children to run their own lives. Parents who persist in bossing the adult children on whom they depend are responsible for the friction they create (Simos, 1973).

Recognition should be given by the children to the irreplaceable nature of the losses experienced by their parents, the way that those losses relate to an unrelievable historical era, and the way that those losses are bound up with their parents' sense of self. At the same time, parents have an obligation, in the face of their great losses, to extend themselves and to make the emotional effort needed to seek new attachments. What is needed on the part of the parents is chathectic flexibility (Peck, 1968), the ability to direct one's love and energy toward new objects in the environment.

Recognition should also be given by children to the way that the irredeemable nature of their obligation to their parents sets the stage for guilt about whether they are doing enough. The situation is not unlike the guilt that young parents feel about what they owe to their children. In a sense, there is no limit to what you can feel obligated to provide to children, especially if you are an educated, concerned parent. This limitless obligation results in what has been called the Supermom Syndrome. The question, therefore, that many young parents face is: "What is my obligation to my children?" An interesting answer which has been given by the British psychiatrist Winnicott (1965) is that what is required is a "good enough" environment and what is required of parents—and this is particularly relevant to mothers—is to be "good enough" mothers. Not to the Supermoms, simply to be "good enough." In a similar vein, the child with a parent in the home is entitled to his or her own life. What is required is not to provide a total life for the parent, but rather an environment adapted to the parent's level of functioning, in which the parent can lead his or her life. What is required is to provide a "good enough" environment. At the same time, parents are required not to exploit their children. They need to recognize that, though what their children owe them far exceeds what is in the children's power to pay back, using the weapon of guilt is a risky and costly strategy—a strategy which results in unhappiness for all involved.

Finally, children need to recognize that the normal course of family life and of individual life entails change and that part of the change that will have to occur is for them to achieve the developmental task of filial maturity, the capacity to accept their parents' aging and to fulfill the needs for help and support which aging brings about. But even here parents have a reciprocal obligation, and in an odd way have power over an aspect of their child's development even as they become dependent on the child's help. This power is the power to control the course of the development of filial maturity in their children. Without the help of their parents, without the reciprocal development of parental maturity, adult children are powerless to accomplish this important developmental task.

REFERENCES

Atchley, R. & Miller, S. Older people and their families. In C. Eisdorfer (Ed.) *Annual Review of Gerontology and Geriatrics,* 1980, *1,* 337–369.

Bane, M. J. *Here to Stay: American Families in the Twentieth Century.* New York: Basic Books, 1976.

Beland, F. The decision of elderly persons to leave their homes. *Gerontologist,* 1984, *24,* 179–185.

Bengston, V. & Treas, J. The changing family context of mental health and aging. In J. E. Birren and R. B. Sloan (Eds.) *Handbook of Mental Health and Aging.* Englewood Cliffs, N.J., Prentice Hall, 1980.

Blau, Z. S. *Aging in a Changing Society.* Second Ed. New York: Franklin Watts, 1981.

Brody, E. "Women in the Middle" and family help to older people. *The Gerontologist,* 1981, *21,* 471–480.

Cicirelli, V. Adult children and their elderly parents. In T. Brubaker, (Ed.) *Family Relationships in Later Life.* Beverly Hills: Sage, 1983.

Deci, E. L. *The Psychology of Self Determination.* Lexington, MA: Lexington, 1980.

Dowd, J. J. Aging as Exchange: A Preface to a Theory, *Journal of Gerontology, 30,* 1975, 584–594.

Fengler, A., Danigelis, H., & Little, V. Later life satisfaction and household structure: living with others and living alone. *Aging and Society,* 1983, *3,* 357–377.

Fillenbaum, G. & Wallman, L. Change in household composition of the elderly: a
preliminary investigation. *Journal of Gerontology,* 1984, *39,* 342–349.

Gouldner, A. The norm of reciprocity: A preliminary statement. *American Sociological Review,* 1960, *25,* 161–178.

Hendricks, J. & Hendricks, C. D. *Aging in Mass Society.* Second Ed. Cambridge,
MA: Winthrop, 1981.

Janis, I. L. & Leventhal, H. Human reactions to stress. In E. Borgatta and W.
Lambert (Eds.) *Handbook of Personality Theory and Research.* Chicago: Rand
McNally, 1968, 1041–1068.

Kivett, V. & Learner, R. Situational influences on the morale of older rural adults in
child-shared housing: A comparative analysis. *Gerontologist,* 1982, *22,* 100–105.

Laslett, P. Societal development and aging. In R. H. Binstock & E. Shanas (Eds.)
Handbook of Aging and the Social Sciences. New York: Van Nostrand Reinhold,
1976.

Lefcourt, H. H. The function of the illusions of control and freedom. *American
Psychologist,* 1973, *28,* 417–425.

Levison, D. *The Seasons of A Man's Life.* New York: Knopf, 1978.

Lopata, H. *Widowhood in an American City.* Cambridge: Schenkman, 1973.

Lowenthal, M. F., Thurnher, M. & Chiriboga, D. *Four Stages of Life.* San Francisco: Jossey-Bass, 1975.

Mindel, C. Multigenerational family households: Recent trends and implications for
the future. *Gerontologist,* 1979, *19,* 456–463.

Neugarten, B. L. The future and the young-old. *The Gerontologist,* 1975, *15,* Supplement, 4–9.

Peck, R. C. Psychological developments in the second half of life. In B. L. Neugarten (Ed.) *Middle Age and Aging.* Chicago: University of Chicago Press, 1968.

Perlmutter, L. C. & Monty, R. A. The Importance of perceived control: Fact or
fiction. *American Scientist,* 1977, *65,* 759–765.

Rubin, L. *Women of a Certain Age: The Midlife Search for Self.* New York: Harper
& Row, 1979.

Schmale, A. H. Giving up as a final common pathway to changes in health. *Psychosomatic Medicine,* 1971, *8,* 18–28.

Shanas, E. Social myth as hypothesis: The case of the family relations of old people.
Gerontologist, 1979, *19,* 3–9.

Simos, B. Adult children and their aging parents. *Social Work,* 1973, *18,* 78–85.

Treas, J. Family support systems for the aged: Some social and demographic considerations. *Gerontologist,* 1977, *17,* 486–491.

Troll, L. Issues in the study of generations. *Aging and Human Development,* 1970, *1,*
199–218.

Troll, L., Miller, S., Atchley, R. *Families in Later Life.* Belmont, CA: Wadsworth,
1979.

Waller, W. The rating and dating complex. *American Sociological Review,* 1937, *2,*
727–734.

Wicklund, R. A. *Freedom and Reactance.* Potomac, MD: Lawrence Erlbaum, 1974.

Winicott, D. W. *The Maturational Processes and The Facilitating Environment.* New
York: International Universities Press, 1965.

Worchel, S. The effects of three types of arbitrary thwarting on the instigation to
aggresssion. *Journal of Personality,* 1974, *42,* 300–318.

Zimbardo, P. G. The human choice: Individuation, reason, and order versus deindi-
viduation, impulse and chaos. In W. J. Arnold & D. Levine (Eds.) *Nebraska
Symposium on Motivation.* Lincoln, NB: University of Nebraska Press, 1969,
237–307.

Older Adult Caregivers of Developmentally Disabled Household Members: Service Needs and Fulfillment

Michael S. Caserta, MS
J. Richard Connelly, PhD
Dale A. Lund, PhD
James L. Poulton, MS

ABSTRACT. The purpose of this study was to evaluate the extent to which there is a need for formal support services among older caregivers with individuals in their homes who are developmentally disabled or intellectually handicapped (DD/IH). The factors which influenced the fulfillment of such service needs were also explored. Information was obtained from a sample of 198 caregivers ranging in age from 50–84, concerning services needed and received, perceived health, competence, difficulty in locating services, as well as a variety of sociodemographic data. The sample reported a significant need for a number of key services, including housekeeping, home repairs, personal counseling, legal services, and physician's services. Only the identified need of physicians' services was adequately filled. Multiple regression analyses revealed that perceived health was the strongest predictor of need fulfillment among those caregivers 60 years of age or older, while difficulty in locating services and perceived competence were influential in explaining need fulfillment of those caregivers between the ages of 50–59. Implications for public policy and future research are discussed.

Michael S. Caserta (Research Associate), J. Richard Connelly (Associate Director for Education), and Dale A. Lund (Associate Director for Research) are with the Intermountain West Long Term Care Gerontology Center, College of Nursing, University of Utah, Salt Lake City, Utah 84112. James L. Poulton is a doctoral candidate with the Department of Psychology, University of Utah. The study was supported by a grant from the Utah Council for Handicapped and Developmentally Disabled Persons (#82 8376). Staff support was also provided by the Intermountain West Long Term Care Gerontology Center.

35

A sizeable portion of the gerontological literature has focused on the elderly population as care recipients (e.g., Bild & Havighurst, 1976; Diamond et al., 1983; Gelfand et al., 1978; Johnson & Catalano, 1981; Loomis & Williams, 1983; Lopata, 1978; Streib, 1978; Reifler & Eisdorfer, 1980; Zawadski & Ansak, 1983). Evidence also exists that many of the elderly are care providers as well (Crossman et al., 1981; Brody, 1985; Kahana and Felton, 1977). The needs of these older adults are complicated by two additional factors. First, since much of their energy and resources are devoted to caregiving, they have the potential of being subject to an inordinate amount of stress and strain (Robinson, 1983). Second, since they are older, their physical and financial resources may be more limited.

While some attention has been paid to the needs of elders who are developmentally disabled (Janicki & MacEachron, 1984), this study focused on older individuals who are themselves caring for predominantly younger disabled (developmentally disabled or intellectually handicapped—DD/IH) household members. This investigation also has implications for older adults in other caregiving situations as well. It has been predicted that more older adults will assume caregiving responsibilities particularly toward spouses and even older parents given the increase in life expectancy (Mayer & Engler, 1982).

It may be tempting to assume, that these older caregivers are in need of formal support services to bolster and complement the resources they have available. However, important policy decisions regarding caregiver services need to be based upon empirical data, which are at this time, very limited. In addition, it is important to identify specific factors that influence the extent to which the need for formal support services is fulfilled. Previous research has indicated that sociodemographic factors such as age, marital status, and income, as well as health are influential variables in need fulfillment (Kahana et al., 1977; Wan et al., 1982). Goodstein (1981) has postulated that health, in particular, can affect access to needed services, since the mobility of the elderly may be significantly impaired by health concerns.

Wan et al. (1982) suggested that the fulfillment of services needs can also be influenced by the interaction of both socioenvironmental and psychological factors. One such factor was perceived competence, which is measured by the way an individual assesses his/her adeptness in responding to the surrounding environment (Goldfried and D'Zurilla, 1969). Specifically, competence refers to the use of an array of skills (Lawton, 1975) which may range from those that are practical and situation-specific (e.g., doing repairs, giving injections, identifying resources) to ones that are more general and psychosocial in nature (e.g., communication skills, assertiveness). Given the demands associated with caregiving, it has been postulated that competence may have an effect on various aspects of the caregiving role. While investigating the subjective well-being of caregivers, Poulton et al. (1984) found that competence had a significant positive effect upon life satisfaction. On the other hand, no empirical evidence has thus far been found illustrating the effect competence has upon the fulfillment of service needs of a population such as this.

Wan et al. (1982) suggested that services needs may go unmet due to the difficulty associated with locating certain services. Primarily, this is related to the social processes of information dissemination and referral. Stumbo et al. (1982), for example, found that patients will tend to visit their physician if they have psychosocial and/or economic problems and needs because they lack information as to where they might otherwise seek assistance. Physicians are often unaware of the availability of resources and therefore, the caregivers' needs are left insufficiently attended (Cohen et al., 1983).

The caregiver's age is an important consideration in service need fulfillment since entitlements, such as those outlined by the Older Americans Act, generally provide easier access to services for those individuals who are 60 years of age or older. However, empirical research is also warranted to determine if there is a difference between those over and under the age of 60 and to what extent age is related to need fulfillment.

The general purposes of this study, therefore, were to examine what special service needs exist for a sample of older adults who are providing care to a DD/IH household member and to identify specific factors which influence their fulfillment. Particular emphasis was on comparing the differences between those who were 60 years of age or older and those who were not yet 60. The research questions addressed in this study are:

1. To what extent is there a need for formal support services as perceived by older caregivers and how adequately is this need being met?
2. What are the relative contributions of perceived health, competence, and selected sociodemographic factors to the service need fulfillment of older caregivers?
3. Are there differences in the patterns of the relative contributions of these factors when comparing those caregivers who are 60 years of age and older to those who are between the ages of 50–59 years?

METHOD

Sample

The sample consisted of 198 respondents who were caregivers to either developmentally disabled or intellectually handicapped individuals in their homes. All respondents lived in urban areas which largely consisted of the metropolitian area of Salt Lake City, Utah. Ninety-seven percent of the sample were white with the majority being female (87%) and married (75%). The next largest marital category consisted of those who were widowed (21%). The average age of the caregivers was 64 years (range 50–84 years), where 60% of the respondents fell into the 60+ category, while the remaining 40% were between the ages of 50–59. Fifty-three percent of the sample reported an annual income of more than $18,000. Twenty-three percent were retired, 69% had a spouse still working and 33% reported that they were employed (19% full-time; 14% part-time).

Of the DD/IH individuals themselves, 89% were the caregivers' children, 2% were spouses, 6% were other relatives (siblings, grandchildren), and 3% were not members of the caregiver's family. Their average age was 32.7 years with 69% being between the ages of 21 and 40 years.

Procedure

Potential respondents were identified with the help of both public agencies and private nonprofit organizations related to programs for the developmentally disabled. A total of 18 organizations were identified and contacted to request their mailing lists of developmentally disabled clients. These agencies included the State Division of Handicapped Services and Family Services, and advocacy groups such as the Association for Retarded Citizens. Each organization screened their lists to include only those persons whose primary caregivers were known to be age 50 and over. These 218 caregivers were then contacted by letter and phone to inform them of the purpose of the study and to request their participation. All respondents were assured of confidentiality. Only 10% refused participation. Upon their acceptance, an appointment was made for a trained interviewer to visit the respondents at their homes, where the interviews were conducted. Each interview lasted approximately 90 minutes.

Measures

In order to measure both perceived service needs and their fulfillment, the respondents were presented a list of 23 different types of services dealing with economic, emotional, social and physical health matters. They were asked to identify the services that they felt they needed to carry out their caregiving responsibilities. For each need indicated, the respondents were then asked if they were currently receiving a service which filled that need. Using this information, a need fulfillment proportion was calculated for each respondent. The sum of all the needs being met by at least one service was divided by the total number of needs reported. This quotient was then multiplied by 100 to yield a percentage in which 0% was indicative of no needs being met and 100% indicated that the respondent was receiving a service to fulfill each reported need.

Health was measured using a self-rating scale which ranged from 0 (poor health) to 3 (excellent health). Linn and Linn (1980) have found that the self reports of health among the elderly are highly correlated with objective health measures.

In order to assess competence, a scale previously developed by Poulton et al. (1982) was modified to be relevant to an older population. Additional items were added which were situationally specific to one's status as a caregiver. The revised instrument consisted of 30 items, each identifying a particular skill for which the respondents were asked to rate their abilities according to a three-point scale (1 = no ability, 2 = some ability, 3 = great ability). Subsequent analyses of the caregivers' responses to the competence scale indicated high internal consistency (Cronbach's Alpha = .80).

In order to measure the degree of difficulty in locating services, the caregivers were asked to indicate how often they had tried to locate services but were unsuccessful in doing so. Responses were categorized according to a five-point scale (1 indicated no difficulty in locating services, 5 indicated the respondent had often been unable to locate services).

RESULTS

The mean health score for the caregivers in this sample was 1.9 (S.D = 0.7). This value falls between the ratings of "good" and "fair." The possible range for the competence scale was 30–90 in which a higher value indicates greater overall perceived competence. The actual range obtained for this sample was 60–90 (M = 82.8; S.D = 5.3). This indicates that the self-perceived competence level was relatively high for this sample of older caregivers.

Table 1 shows the perceived needs of the caregivers with respect to each of the services listed as well as the proportions who received the needed service versus those who did not. The services for which the highest percentages of caregivers reported a need were doctor's care (45.5%), lawyer's services (44.4%), personal counseling (31.3%), housekeeping (22.2%), and home repairs (21.2%).

The least needed services were counseling related to problems with neighbors (1.5%), finding volunteer work (1.5%), finding new residence, job training, and physical aids (all 2.0%). It is interesting to note that all 23 services were needed by at least three of the caregivers. This underscores the multiplicity and diversity of their needs.

Most caregivers who reported the need for a physician found access to that service (92.2%). On the other hand, 70.5% who reported the need for a lawyer had not been successful in attaining this type of service. Among these caregivers the need for a lawyer was reported second only to that of a physician. Also striking is how unsuccessful the sample had been in locating assistance in housekeeping and home repairs in which 81%

Table 1

Caregiver Needs and Services Received

Service	Service Needed (N)	%	Service Received (N)	%	Service Needed But Not Received (N)	%
Housekeeping	(44)	22.2	(7)	15.9	(37)	84.1
Home Repairs	(42)	21.2	(8)	19.0	(34)	81.0
Personal Counseling	(62)	31.3	(25)	40.3	(37)	59.7
Family Counseling	(38)	19.2	(12)	31.6	(26)	68.4
Counseling Re: Problems with Neighbors	(3)	1.5	(0)	0.0	(3)	100.0
Doctor's Care	(90)	45.5	(83)	92.2	(7)	7.8
Nursing Care	(14)	7.1	(8)	57.1	(6)	42.9
Physical Therapy	(26)	13.1	(8)	30.8	(18)	69.2
Social Club/Group	(33)	16.7	(16)	48.5	(17)	51.5
Recreation/Hobby Club	(28)	14.1	(10)	35.7	(18)	64.3
Meals Brought	(21)	10.6	(1)	4.8	(20)	95.2
Comfortable Sleeping Place	(5)	2.5	(2)	40.0	(3)	60.0
Transportation	(20)	10.1	(3)	15.0	(17)	85.0
Regular Contact	(14)	7.1	(7)	50.0	(7)	50.0
Assistance in Finding New Residence	(4)	2.0	(0)	0.0	(4)	100.0
Lawyer Services	(88)	44.4	(26)	29.5	(62)	70.5
Guardian/Power of Attorney	(11)	5.6	(4)	36.4	(7)	63.6
Finding Paid Employment	(10)	5.1	(2)	20.0	(8)	80.0
Finding Volunteer Work	(3)	1.5	(1)	53.3	(2)	66.7
Job Training (if handicapped)	(4)	2.0	(1)	25.0	(3)	60.0
Physical Aids	(4)	2.0	(1)	25.0	(3)	75.0
Service Organization and Arrangement	(37)	18.7	(2)	5.4	(35)	94.6
Other Needs	(18)	9.1	(4)	22.2	(14)	77.8

were unable to locate assistance doing needed repairs on their home while 84.1% were also unsuccessful in obtaining assistance in the general upkeep of their home.

In the area of personal counseling, many caregivers reported some success in fulfilling their perceived needs, yet those who were not successful (59.7%) still outnumbered those who were (40.3%). Although not among the five services with the most reported need, the need for family counseling was reported by a number of caregivers (19.2%). However, of the 38 respondents who identified such a need 26 (68.4%) reported receiving no such service.

Some caregivers reported the need for a service or program that could provide them access to a club or group for either recreational (14.1%) or socializing (16.7%) purposes. Of the respondents who wished to join a social club, 51.5% reported that no such group was available to them. Similarly, 64.3% of those who wished to join a club or group for the purpose of recreation or hobbies were also lacking in such an access.

The amount of need reported by the sample pertaining to certain outreach services (such as meals brought, transportation assistance, and regular contact) was quite low. This is probably a function of the fact that many of the caregivers were still quite mobile, with generally fair to good health.

Also low in priority regarding need were employment related services. This is not surprising given that most of the caregivers were either employed themselves or married to a spouse who was employed. Thirty-seven caregivers (18.7%), however, did report a need for a program to organize all their service needs and then make arrangements for them to receive needed services. Similar to the patterns observed for most of the other service needs only 5.4% of the respondents reported this as available.

The analyses pertaining to the factors associated with need fulfillment were conducted separately for those caregivers 60 years of age and older and those between the ages of 50–59 years. Tables 2 and 3 show the distributions of the need fulfillment proportion for those two age groups.

Table 2 shows that nearly 52% of the 60+ caregivers had a need fulfillment proportion of 50% or greater, but 25% of this age group had from 0 to 9% of their needs filled. These percentages indicate that there was a great deal of variation in the

Table 2

Need Fulfillment for Caregivers Age 60 and Over

Need Fulfillment Percentage	N	Percent[a]
0- 9	26	25.0
10-19	3	2.9
20-29	7	6.7
30-39	10	9.6
40-49	4	3.9
50-59	24	23.1
60-69	5	4.8
70-79	4	3.9
80-89	--	--
90-99	1	1.0
100	20	19.2

Median = 49.5

[a] Percent may not total 100.0 due to rounding

need fulfillment of these older caregivers. Table 3 shows that the rates were generally lower for the under 60 age group. Approximately one-half of these caregivers had a need fulfillment proportion of 29% or less (median = 29.2), including 35.7% who were in the 0–9% category. It is also noteworthy to mention that both age groups had a similar amount of caregivers whose need fulfillment percentage equaled 100 (60+ = 19.2%; under 60 = 21.4%). This indicates that there are caregivers within each group whose needs are being totally met. These are most likely the respondents whose amount of perceived needs were generally lower than the rest of the sample.

In order to determine which factors were most influential in determining the amount of need fulfillment for each age group, selected variables needed to be entered into a step-wise multiple regression analysis. To rule out extraneous effects, a series of one-way analyses of variance (ANOVA) were performed on need fulfillment within each age group using marital status, gender, and ethnicity as independent variables. No sta-

Table 3

Need Fulfillment for Caregivers Under Age 60

Need Fulfillment Percentage	N	Percent[a]
0- 9	25	35.7
10-19	5	7.1
20-29	5	7.1
30-39	5	7.1
40-49	1	1.4
50-59	7	10.0
60-69	1	1.4
70-79	3	4.3
80-89	3	4.3
90-99	--	--
100	15	21.4

Median = 29.2

[a] Percent may not total 100.0 due to rounding.

tistically significant effects were found. The variables that were ultimately entered into the regression analyses, therefore, were perceived health, perceived competence, difficulty in locating services, income, caregiver age, and DD/IH age. Although the effect of age was at least partially controlled by treating the two groups separately, caregiver age was allowed to remain in the analyses because of its possible relationship to other variables. Age of the DD/IH household member was also entered into the analyses for similar reasons, since it might be part of the eligibility criteria for some programs.

Table 4 shows the result of the step-wise regression performed on the 60+ age group. The only factor which proved to have a significant influence on the amount of need fulfillment was perceived health of the caregiver ($p < .05$): a higher health rating had a positive impact on the fulfillment of service needs. This variable alone contributed 11.5% of the variance in need fulfillment. The insignificance of the remaining variables shows that once the effect of perceived health is controlled, their influence—for this age group—is diminished.

In contrast, perceived health of the caregiver was one of the least significant variables predicting need fulfillment in the under 60 age group. Table 5 shows that difficulty in locating services (p < .05) as well as perceived competence (p < .05) were the most influential factors, together explaining 13.5% of the variance. While increased difficulty in locating services had a negative impact on need fulfillment, a higher perceived competence rating tended to affect it in a positive way. It is interesting to note that these two factors were the least significant in explaining need fulfillment for the 60+ age group. Therefore, the factors that influence the caregivers' need fulfillment are different for those under the age of 60 and those age 60 and over.

DISCUSSION

This study examined three research questions pertaining to the service needs of older caregivers. The first question addressed the extent to which a need for formal support services exists. The relative contribution of selected variables to the fulfillment of perceived needs was also examined with particu-

Table 4

Regression Summary Table: Selected Variables
On Need Fulfillment (60+)

Variables	Simple R	Multiple R^a	R^{2a}	Unstandardized b
Perceived Health of Caregiver	.34	.34	.115	14.20*
Age of Caregiver	-.19	.38	.143	-.97
Age of DD/IH	.09	.39	.152	.24
Income	.13	.40	.158	1.15
Competence	.14	.40	.161	.35
Difficulty Locating Services	-.07	.40	.163	-1.11

*p < .05

[a] Cumulative as of each step.

Table 5

Regression Summary Table: Selected
Variables On Need Fulfillment (Under 60)

Variables	Simple R	Multiple R[a]	R^{2a}	Unstandardized b
Difficulty Locating Services	-.27	.27	.073	-7.52*
Competence	.23	.37	.135	2.31*
Age of Caregiver	-.08	.40	.152	-1.85
Age of DD/IH	-.04	.41	.166	-.48
Perceived Health of Caregiver	.16	.41	.169	3.67
Income	.05	.41	.171	-1.13

*p < .05

[a] Cumulative as of each step.

lar emphasis on observing any differences between those care-givers aged 50–59 years and those who were older (60+).

The findings indicate that a significant proportion of the older caregivers in this study reported a need for key services aimed at alleviating the stress and strain associated with caring for a person in their home that is developmentally disabled or intellectually handicapped. For the most part, with the exception of those services rendered by a physican, these needs have gone largely unmet.

Although some of the respondents were located using social service agency lists, these lists were primarily those of handicapped services, not services specifically aimed at the caregivers. Even though some of the DD/IH individuals were receiving a service (for instance, physical therapy), it does not necessarily follow that the caregiver would be receiving any direct service as well. Furthermore, in a number of cases, even the DD/IH individual was no longer receiving services even though his/her name may have appeared on this list.

Some of the reported needs may be unique to the caregiving situation. For example, these caregivers may be particularly concerned for the future welfare of the DD/IH individual in their households (e.g., wills/trusts, future arrangements for care). This may explain the sizeable presence of the need for a lawyer's services. In addition, the majority of the respondents who reported needs concerning home maintenance (whether it be repair work or general upkeep), received no such service. The demand for this service is understandable given the potential for difficulty in addressing the needs of a DD/IH household member, which may often require such an amount of time that household duties cannot often be fully attended. This issue becomes more important as the caregivers get older since poor physical health was related to unmet needs. Finally, it is also not surprising that given the possibility for caregiver stress particularly when caring for an individual who may be handicapped, there is a reported need for professional counseling. An increasing amount of research has found beneficial effects in terms of enhanced coping skills and support as a result of this kind of service (Zarit, 1985). It appears evident that efforts must be made to increase the availability of mental health services for caregivers to help them to cope with the demands associated with the caregiving role.

Differences in need fulfillment were found when comparing those caregivers who were 60 years of age or older with those who were between the ages of 50–59. The only factor predictive of need fulfillment for those 60 years of age and older was their perceived health. This is consistent with previous findings concerning the fulfillment of service needs for the elderly population in general, especially considering the relationship that health has with mobility (Goodstein, 1981). If mobility is impaired due to poor health access to needed services can be limited.

There was nothing exceptionally distinctive about this set of caregivers upon comparison with other findings concerning service utilization and need fulfillment. If anything is surprising at all, it is the lack of predictive power associated with the factors other than perceived health. This may be attributed to a decreased amount of variability in factors such as income, in which the sample was fairly homogeneous, and age whose variability was diminished by analyzing the age groups separately.

Caution is advised regarding the overall generalizability of the study findings because of the relative homogeneity of the sample since they were primarily white, middle class, and married. It should be noted, however, that many other caregivers have similar characteristics and therefore, have similar service needs. Many of these services are entitlements outlined in the Older American's Act which apply to all those over age 60. Although some of the limitations due to sampling may detract from the generalizability of these findings, the extent of service needs found in this study is probably, if anything, underestimated, since those in greater need, with no ties to the social service network, may have been missed. Further research into other subpopulations of elderly caregivers can test this contention. In doing so, specific emphasis should perhaps be placed on those in frail health.

Regarding those caregivers who are below the age of 60, the problem is a different one. First, the analysis revealed that a sizeable segment of this group have service needs which are mostly unmet. This group is subject to the predicament of being in a "service gap" as illustrated by their difficulty in locating services. This can result from two possible factors. Their age makes them ineligible for entitlements outlined by the Older Americans' Act and by virtue of the age of the DD/IH person in their home, they are also not eligible for a number of other programs because many entitlements are no longer received once the DD/IH individual reaches 21 years of age.

It is also important to emphasize, however, that the amount of need fulfillment for this age group is not solely dependent upon eligibility criteria. While difficulty in locating services (and its subsequent effect on need fulfillment) may partly be a function of the "service gap" phenomenon, there is also evidence that competence, which includes such factors as the ability to identify resources, is influential as well. It should be noted that the competency levels were relatively high for this sample. On the other hand, it is possible that competence in particular skills (such as the ability to identify resources, the utilization of both public and private modes of transportation, being assertive, and so on) may be more directly related to service access. Caregivers who are adept in these skills might be more successful in fulfilling their service needs. More quantitative and qualitative research on the competency of older caregivers is needed to understand this relationship.

Another direction for future research lies in the search for additional factors that are related to need fulfillment. While this study has yielded some useful information as to the relative contributions of selected sociodemographic variables as well as perceived health and competence, a large amount of the variance in need fulfillment still remains unexplained. Research into the role of such factors as informal support networks, ethnicity, and other cultural traits of the older caregiver may significantly add to these findings.

Finally, it is relatively clear that a need exists for greater service access and more effective information dispersal. Our findings indicate that it would be particularly beneficial to educate the health care community as to what resources are available to fill needs which are not strictly biomedical. Since it is apparent that the access to a doctor's care is the one service need that is filled fairly adequately, physicians would seem to be a suitable source through whom service information can be disseminated. Investigations into cost effective strategies are therefore recommended and encouraged.

REFERENCES

Bild, B.R. & Havighurst, R.H. (1976). Family and social support, chapter VIII. *The Gerontologist, 16,* 63–69.

Brody, E. M. (1985). Parent care as normative family stress. *The Gerontologist, 25,* 19–29.

Cohen, D. Hegarty, J., & Eisdorfer, C. (1983). The desk directory of social resources: A physicians reference guide to social and community services for the aged. *Journal of the American Geriatrics Society, 31,* 338–341.

Crossman, L., London, C., & Barrie, C. (1981). Older women caring for disabled spouses: A model for supportive services. *The Gerontologist, 21,* 464–470.

Diamond, L.M., Gruenberg, L. & Morris, R.L. (1983). Elder care for the 1980s: Health and social service in one prepaid health maintenance system. *The Gerontologist, 23,* 148–154.

Gelfand, D.E., Olsen, J.K., & Block, M.R. (1978). Two generations of elderly in the changing American family: Implications for family services. *The Family Coordinator, 27,* 395–403.

Goldfried, M.R. & D'Zurilla, T.J. (1969). A behavior-analytic model for assessing competence. In C.D. Spielberger (Ed.), *Current Topics in Clinical and Community Psychology,* (Vol. 1). New York: Academic Press.

Goodstein, R.K. (1981). Inextricable interaction: Social, psychologic, and biologic stresses facing the elderly. *American Journal of Orthopsychiatry, 51,* 219–229.

Janicki, M.P. & MacEachron, A.E. (1984). Residential, health, and social service needs of elderly developmentally disabled persons. *The Gerontologist, 24,* 128–137.

Johnson, C.L. & Catalano, D.J. (1981). Childless elderly and their family supports. *The Gerontologist, 21,* 610–618.

Kahana, E. & Felton, B. (1977). Social context and personal needs—a study of Polish and Jewish aged. *Journal of Social Issues, 33* (4), 56–74.

Kahana, E., Liang, J., Felton, B., Fairchild, T., & Harel, Z. (1977). Perspectives of aged on victimization, "ageism," and their problems in urban society. *The Gerontologist, 17,* 121–129.

Lawton, M.P. (1975). Competence, environmental press, and the adaptation of older people. In T.G. Windley, T.O. Byerts, & F.G. Ernst (eds.), *Theory Development in Environment and Aging.* Manhattan, Kansas: Gerontological Society.

Linn, B.S., & Linn, M.W. (1980). Objective and self-assessed health in the old and very old. *Social Science and Medicine, 14A,* 311–315.

Loomis, M.T. & Williams, T.F. (1983). Evaluation of care provided to terminally ill patients. *The Gerontologist, 23,* 493–499.

Lopata, H.Z. (1978). The absence of community resources in support systems of urban widows. *The Family Coordinator, 27,* 383–388.

Mayer, M.J. & Engler, M. (1982). Demographic change and the elderly population: Its implications for long term care. *Pride Institute Journal of Long Term Home Health Care, 1,* 21–28.

Poulton, J.L., Connelly, J.R., Caserta, M.S. & Lund, D.A. (1984). The older caregiver: Competence, social supports and life satisfaction. Paper presented at the annual meeting of the Western Gerontological Society, Anaheim, California.

Poulton, J.L., Paul, S.C., & Ostrow, E. (1982). Personal competence: Conceptualization, measurement, and preventive implications. Paper presented at the annual meeting of the American Psychological Association, Washington, D.C.

Riefler, B.V. & Eisdorfer, C. (1980). A clinic for the impaired elderly and their families. *American Journal of Psychiatry, 137,* 1399–1403.

Robinson, B.C. (1983). Validation of a caregiver strain index. *Journal of Gerontology, 38,* 344–348.

Streib, G.F. (1978). An alternative family form for older persons: Need and social context. *The Family Coordinator, 27,* 413–420.

Stumbo, D., Delvecchio-Good, M., & Good, B.J. (1982). A diagnostic profile of a family practice clinic: Patients with psychosocial diagnoses. *Journal of Family Practice, 14,* 281–285.

Wan, T.T.H., Odell, B.G., & Lewis, D.T. (1982). *Promoting the Well-Being of the Elderly: A Community Diagnosis.* New York: The Haworth Press.

Zarit, S.H. (1985). New directions. *Generations, 10* (1), 6–8.

Zawadski, R.T. & Ansak, M. (1983). Consolidating community-based long-term care: Early returns from the On Lok demonstration. *The Gerontologist, 23,* 364–369.

Intervention With Families of the Elderly Chronically Ill: An Alternate Approach

Margaret R. Rodway
Joyce Elliott
Russel J. Sawa

ABSTRACT. A workshop format for addressing the needs of families of the institutionalized chronically ill is described as an alternate approach to social work intervention. The organization and development of the family workshop is reviewed and its process commented on in terms of phases. An evaluation of the workshop by family members suggested that the major benefits of the workshop for the families were: a sharing and increased understanding of the family members' feelings; a beginning clarification of communication patterns in the family; an elucidation of family expectations of the extended care facility staff; a better understanding of the importance of staff-family relationships; and finally increased information on the dynamics and aspects of chronic illness. Recommendations concerning the nature and format of family workshops are provided.

INTRODUCTION

Chronic illness is often a massive assault on family stability and health, leading to many potential problems. Family reaction to illness is frequently discussed in the literature (Olsen, 1970; Mailick, 1979; Krupp, 1976; Bruhn, 1977; Levenstein, 1980; Burr, 1978). Those at risk are identified (Livsey, 1972) as well as those who cope well (Scatterwhite, 1970; Anthony,

---

Margaret R. Rodway is on the faculty of Social Welfare, The University of Calgary, 2500 University Drive N. W., Calgary, Alberta, 42N, IN4, Canada. Joyce Elliott is with the Department of Social Work, Bethany Care Centre; and Russell J. Sawa is on the faculty of Medicine, the University of Calgary.

1969). Families may respond to illness by growth, temporary breakdown or disintegration (Stein, 1980; Binger, 1969). Illness can be a burden to families (Scatterwhite, 1970) and cause change in function such as status of members, sexual activity between parents, discipline and household duties (Binger, 1969; Koski and Jumento, 1977). In families of the elderly who are chronically ill, these reactions are often identified.

In particular, placement of a family member in an extended care facility is very stressful and difficult for the patient and the family itself. The impact of chronic illness on both institutionalized patient and family has been examined in a number of articles.

Cook (1981) concluded that:

> upon admission to a long term care facility, persons are both physically and emotionally separated from family and friends. Emotional support is crucial in aiding adjustment, yet regular visitation by family members may be difficult due to the location of the extended care facility or because of family unresolved guilt feelings regarding the placement.

Shanas (1979) has observed that "no matter what the extenuating circumstances, the older person who has children interprets the move to an institution as rejection by his children." He asserts moreover that even the family that has had good relationships, may find the process of institutionalization evokes feelings of pain, sorrow, loss and guilt. Robinson & Thurner (1979) suggest that the family often experiences the stress of perceived mental deterioration of a family member prior to institutionalization which may result in a negative portrayal of that member and subsequent family withdrawal.

Given the difficulties experienced by both families and patients in extended care facilities, social work intervention is crucial, so that the variety of negative effects can be lessened and the family's potential to become a major source of help (Brody, 1978) can be enhanced. Indeed Romney (1962) has suggested that the future of these family-patient relationships often will depend on the previous quality of family relationships, the acceptance of placement and the services of the institution. As institutional care providers increasingly recognize the importance of the family in effective patient care, the development of appropriate intervention addressed to meeting family needs is essential.

The literature is limited in terms of describing the type of social work services offered in extended care to address these issues. Greene (1982) refers to the variety of clinical interventions that could be used for enhancing family relationships which might be utilized: individual casework, family therapy and discussion groups. Solomon (1982) describes direct intervention with both patient and family around four stages of institutional extended care: the decision to enter; the actual entry; the move to a more intensive level of care and the death of the patient. A different direction to clinical interventions is provided by Safford's (1976) training program for families of patients in extended care facilities as well as in the community. Her program was developed to help families

> recognize the universal elements in their unique situations, while attempting to help them work through developmental tasks so that they could appropriately accept being depended on by their kin. The 12 hour program over a six week period transmitted knowledge about mental impairment, aging and the attitudes that affect the skills needed to provide proper care, as well as the opportunity to discuss individual problems.

One of the major problems in offering clinical interventions in extended care is the cost in terms of time and money for the social work staff. As well, many families are hesitant to engage in a counselling relationship, as they view themselves as healthy, functioning families. While clinical intervention may be the desired type of service in many instances, optional approaches such as that described by Safford should be developed so that a range of interventions is available. New and creative ideas need to be developed to respond to the needs of families of the chronically ill, particularly the elderly segment of this population. This article will describe a workshop format as an alternate approach to clinical intervention with families experiencing the impact of chronic illness.

FAMILY WORKSHOP DESCRIPTION

The workshop was initiated within the extended care facility, not in terms of reducing costs of social work services, but rather to meet the needs of a particular group of families, who either didn't see the need for social work services or were hesitant to directly request needed assistance. Usually these families had always dealt with their own issues within the family and wished to continue to do so. As well, many of the families in the study were from middle or upper middle class backgrounds and therefore the concept of an educational-type workshop appealed to them based on their previous life experience. While self-help groups are gaining increased use in terms of providing support to those who see this need, this format was seen as a structure from which participants could begin to increase their understanding of their concerns, and gain some new concepts and ideas on how to cope with these concerns which could subsequently be used on their own. In essence, the workshop approach gave the families credit for having good problem-solving skills as well as helping them deal with issues of preventative nature.

There were a number of steps involved in the organization of the workshop. First, it was necessary to gain the support of the administration of the extended care facility in order to pursue an innovative approach to social work involvement. This was followed by the selection and recruitment of two other professionals, a family physician and social worker-psychologist, who would assist the director of social work services in leading the workshop. It was decided to have inter-professional leaders in order to provide a breadth of input to the participants in the workshop. The family physician's input was directed primarily toward descriptive information on the nature of chronic illness and the phases of response to such illness. The social worker and psychologist provided information on family functioning and response to change; coping mechanisms and emotional reactions to chronic illness.

A three hour duration for the workshop was decided upon based on a number of factors. There was a wish to maintain a time limited nature to the workshop which is consistent with this type of activity. This length of time easily comprised an afternoon session, following which families were able to visit their patient-members and assist them over the meal time. Finally the length of time of the workshop was checked out informally with a number of families who were most receptive to this length than others suggested.

It was also necessary to select and train small group facilitators. The eight leaders were chosen from the health care staff of the extended facility on the basis of their skills with groups and their sensitivity to group needs. In terms of training, initially the focus for group leaders was on stimulating their interest, motivation and enthusiasm for the workshop. The second aspect was to provide a structure for the group process: i.e., to facilitate introductions of the group members and then to arrange for the group to develop vignettes related to chronic illness. The group leaders were also encouraged to be flexible in terms of group process and to encourage sharing of concerns by group members. The final step was to invite the seventy-one families suggested by the facility health team and director of social services, as those who would benefit from such an experience based on the rationale discussed previously. As a result of this process, thirty-four families attended the workshop. Those families who were invited but did not attend indicated that either they lived out of town or worked during the day and hence were unable to participate.

During the actual workshop, the time was divided between two segments; first, one hour in small group discussions and then two hours talking together as a large group. Initially, each small group was asked to prepare two vignettes that expressed some of the concerns or issues related to chronic illness within families. It was explained that these vignettes would be used as the basis for the workshop discussion and that the workshop leaders would dialogue with the participants around these narratives and in this way address their concerns. The format of the workshop was casual and fairly unstructured in order to maximize peer learning and to enable the leaders to respond directly to the needs of the group.

Group Process

During the first segment of the workshop, the small group discussions, the major emphasis was on sharing and exploring the issues and concerns related to chronic illness within families, which the participants had identified. This aspect enabled participants to realize that others shared similar concerns and that they were not alone with their problems. The small group facilitators encouraged and supported the group in their discussions.

In the second phase of the workshop, the leaders, functioning as a panel, responded to the small group examples from the family situations and facilitated large group determination of solutions. This process was enhanced by helping the group more clearly define the problem or problems (which often had been left at a very vague level, as is frequently seen in families who are having problems coping), then to define the support system by clarifying who is in the family and outlining what solutions have been attempted, and then to come up with new possible solutions. Often the more significant issues, usually emotional relationship aspects (i.e., fear of not being loved, feelings of guilt, fear of abandonment) were not clearly defined as a problem. Instrumental issues were often identified and focussed on instead of these more difficult issues. The participants were able to recognize that these steps, along with discussion in a supportive context, was helpful and productive.

Feelings of hopelessness in overwhelming situations led to a discussion of the importance of evaluating the meaning of one's life experience as being a helpful coping mechanism. Issues such as institutionalization and degeneration of the personality of the ill member illustrated such situations. The emphasis in filling one's own needs in order to be effective was highlighted. The fact that giving in to feelings of hopelessness can lead to mental and physical illness was discussed. Ineffective coping mechanisms, such as avoidance, alcohol and drugs, and blaming were mentioned.

The workshop leaders encouraged the group to express feelings about their situation and to share those feelings. Confusion, anxiety, resentment, guilt, and feelings of hopelessness were identified. Participants were encouraged to reach out to group members for support. The fact that these feelings were normal was emphasized, as well as the fact that they represented attempts at coping.

The response to illness was discussed. The fact that individual responses to chronic illness pass through various stages was outlined. The first of these stages is denial, then confu-

sion, anxiety and resentment, and finally recovery and/or re-
organization and acceptance. The various feelings experienced are comparable to those outlined by Kübler-Ross
(1969).

Finally, the importance of using the family of origin as a
support group, and improving it by adult-adult relationships
was highlighted. Finding a balance, and connecting with
others were also encouraged.

Workshop Evaluation

At the conclusion of the workshop, the participants were
requested to complete a simple rating scale. The results of
their ratings are shown in Table 1.

It should be noted that seventy-four percent of the families
gave top rating to the format of the workshop and ninety-six
percent indicated they would be interested in attending another. Some additional comments from the group were "more
time please," "could be held in the evenings so more family
members could attend," "the discussions were low key, easy
and very revealing," "all of us attending are here because we

FAMILY EVALUATION OF WORKSHOP

Rating			1	2	3	4	5	TOTAL
1.	SUBJECT	(a)	Interesting		Not so interesting			
	MATERIAL	Frequency	20	2	2	0		24*
		Percentage	84	8	8	0		100
		(b)	Relevant		Not so relevant			
		Frequency	12	4	2	1		19**
		Percentage	64	21	10	5		100
2.	PANEL		Good			Poor		
	PRESENTATION	Frequency	15	7	1	1		24
		Percentage	62	30	4	4		100
3.	FORMAT OF		Good			Poor		
	WORKSHOP	Frequency	17 ·	3	2	1		23***
		Percentage	75	13	8	4		100

* While 34 families participated in the workshop, 10 had to leave early, prior
to the completion of the questionnaire.

** 5 families did not complete this question.

*** 1 family did not complete this question.

need this kind of meeting," "the feeling of not being adequate to cope with our situation must be universal" and "please have more workshops so we can follow up our gains made here. Helping us to help others is helping us and we plead for it."

Examples of some of the more negative comments were: would like more assistance in following up daily problems; more time required; more individual and personal attention could be given if the group was smaller.

CONCLUSIONS AND RECOMMENDATIONS

A workshop for families of the chronically ill in an extended care facility has been described. It was developed as an alternate approach to direct intervention with families, and could be viewed as part of a range of social work interventive services. The response of the families to the workshop was favourable and from these it was concluded that the major benefits of the workshop for the participants were: a sharing and beginning understanding of the family members feelings of anguish, fear, pity, sadness and resentment; some clarification of communication patterns in the family; an elucidation of family expectations of the extended care facility staff; a better understanding of the importance of staff-family relationships; and finally, increased information on the dynamics and aspects of chronic illness. However, it should be noted that these conclusions regarding gains by the participants in fact represent a starting point for some of these issues to be further addressed within the families. The crucial nature of some of these benefits have been supported in the literature (Farkas, 1980; Montgomery, 1983; Shuttleworth, Rubin and Duff, 1982).

For those who are interested in organizing a similar family workshop, there are a number of aspects of the format which could remain the same. The size of the group appeared to be optimal; the small group discussion was helpful in itself and later encouraged dialogue between the panel and families. The interdisciplinary nature of the panel added a breadth to the information provided. In directing the families to small groups, they were encouraged not to sit with friends or individuals they knew previously. Feedback from participants indicated that being with strangers enabled them to express feelings more easily.

There are, however, some changes that could be incorporated. First, the initial small group task could be different. Rather than preparing vignettes as a group, it is suggested that initially they share information about themselves and then as a group came up with a number of specific questions for the leaders about the issues that families with a chronically ill member might face. This would provide the leaders with a much clearer sense of direction as to how to formulate their subsequent comments. Second, there would also be merit in extending the time that families spend in the small groups. Possibly after the leaders had provided their response to the large group, the families could return to the small groups to process the information. This would also facilitate its application to their specific situations. Third, the workshop could also be scheduled during the evening so that those family members who are employed during the daytime, could also attend. Finally, the workshop is an opportune time to initiate the formation of an ongoing support group. Families who might otherwise be resistive to such an idea would be more receptive and motivated to commit themselves to group counselling after being part of a family workshop. In the present study, it should be noted that some of the participants did become part of existing support groups. As well, others requested individual sessions with the social work staff. The workshop then served an additional function of identifying and meeting needs which might not otherwise have occurred.

REFERENCES

Anthony, E.J. "The Mutative Impact on Family Life of Serious Mental and Physical Illness in a Parent." *Canadian Psychiatry Association Journal,* 14, 1969, 433–453.

Binger, C.M., Ablin, A.R., Feurstein, R.C., Kushner, G.H., Zoger, S., and Mikkelsen, C. "Childhood Leukemea: Emotional Impact on Patient and Family." *New England Journal of Medicine,* February 20, 1969, pp. 414–418.

Brody, E., Poulschoeck, W. and Mascobi, C. "The Family Caring Unit: A Major Consideration in the Long-Term Care Support System." *The Gerontologist,* 18(6), 1978, pp. 556–561.

Bruhn, J.G. "Effects of Chronic Illness on the Family." *Journal of Family Practice,* 4(6), 1977, 1057–1077.

Burr, B.D., Good, B.J., and Good, M. "The Impact of Illness on the Family." In R.B. Taylor (ed.), *Family Medicine Principles and Practice*. New York: Springer-Verlag, 1978, 221–233.

Cook, A.S. "A Model for Working With the Elderly in Institutions." *Social Casework*, 62(7), 1981, pp. 420–425.

Farkas, S.W. "Impact of Chronic Illness on the Patient's Spouse." *Health and Social Work*, 5(4), 1980, pp. 38–57.

Greene, R.R. "Families and the Nursing Home Social Worker." *Social Work in Health Care*, 7(3), 1982, pp. 57–67.

Koski, M.L. and Jumento, A. "The Interrelationship Between Diabetic Control and Family Life." *Pediatric Adolescent Endocrinol.*, 3, 1977, pp. 41–45.

Krupp, N.E. "Adaptation to Chronic Illness." *Post Graduate Medicine.*, 60, July–Dec, 1976.

Kübler-Ross, E. *Death and Dying*. New York: Macmillan, 1969.

Levenstein, S. "The Psychological Management of the Patient with Chronic Illness and His Family." *S. African Medical Journal*, 57(10), March, 1980, pp. 361–362.

Livsey, C.G. "Physical Illness Family Dynamics: Advanced Psychosomatic Medicine." Kraeger, Basel, *Advances in Psychosomatic Medicine*, Vol. 8, 1972, pp. 237–251.

Mailick, M. *Social Work in Health Care*, 5(2). Haworth Press, 1979.

Montgomery, R.J.V. "Staff-Family Relations and Institutional Care Policies." *Journal of Gerontological Social Work*, 6(1), 1983, pp. 25–37.

Olsen, E.H. "The Impact of Serious Illness on the Family System." *Post Graduate Medicine*, February 1970, pp. 169–174.

Robinson, B. and Thurner, M. "Taking Care of Aged Parents: A Family Cycle Transition." *The Gerontologist*, 19(6), 1979, pp. 586–593.

Romney, L. "Extension of Family Relationships Into a Home for the Aged." *Social Work*, 7, 1962, 31–34.

Safford, F. "A Training Program For Families of the Mentally Impaired Aged as Linkage Mechanism in a System of Care." City University of New York D.S.W., September, 1976.

Scatterwhite, B.B. "Impact of Chronic Illness on Child and Family: An Overview Based on Five Surveys with Complications for Management." *International Journal of Rehabilitation Research*, 1970, pp. 7–17.

Shanas, E. "The Family as a Social System in Old Age." *The Gerontologist*, 19(2), 1979, pp. 169–174.

Shuttleworth, G.E., Rubin, A. and Duff, M. "Families Versus Institutions: Incongruent Role Expectations in the Nursing Home." *The Gerontologist*, 22(2), 1982, pp. 200–208.

Solomon, R. "Serving Families of the Institutionalized Age: The Four Crises." *Journal of Gerontological Social Work*, 5(1/2), 1982, pp. 83–96.

Stein, et al. "The Development of an Impact on the Family Scale: Preliminary Findings." *Medical Care*, XVIII(4), April, 1980.

The Family and Dependency: Factors Associated With Institutional Decision-Making

Judith G. Gonyea, PhD

ABSTRACT. This research investigated the planning by family members for the institutionalization of their elderly relatives. Institutional decision-making was conceptualized as having four stages: recognition; discussion; implementation; and placement. The key question explored was what are the most salient structural and dynamic factors associated with the first three stages of institutional decision-making, and do these critical factors vary with each stage. Multivariate analyses revealed that both sets of variables make independent contributions to the prediction of the caregiver's involvement in each stage of decision-making. The implications of the findings for future research and practice are discussed.

While the presence of a strong family network is often a deterrent to institutionalization, fully 76 percent of institutionalized elderly report having family (USDHHS, 1981). In fact, when a family network does exist the decision to institutionalize a vulnerable older person is often a family process (Lieberman, 1978). Montgomery and Borgatta (1982) suggest that families seek to institutionalize their aged relatives when they perceive an incongruence between their own resources and the needs of the aged person. Family members are, thus, actors of considerable importance in the decision to institutionalize an older dependent relative.

To date, the majority of studies examining factors influencing the institutionalization of older persons have treated placement as an outcome or product variable. These research studies can generally be categorized in two groups: those

---

Dr. Gonyea is Assistant Professor, Boston University School of Social Work, 264 Bay State Road, Boston, MA 02215.

61

studies comparing selected characteristics of the institutionalized elderly with either the general elderly population or elderly residing in the community (Barney, 1977; Vincente et
al., 1979); and those studies examining factors associated with
the family's placement of an aged relative in a nursing home
either at the point of, or after admission (Brody, 1966; Kraus
et al., 1976; Dobrof, 1976). One exception has been Teresi's
(1978) prospective study of family attitudes towards institutionalizing older relatives.

Common to most of these studies is the focus on the final
point or outcome of institutional decision-making, when institutionalization has become a *fait accompli.* Yet the clinical
gerontological literature has repeatedly documented that the
placement of an older person in an institution is not a brief or
simple process. Families usually undertake a series of attempts to resolve the older person's problems prior to institutionalization. The nursing home is viewed as the last resort by
both the aged and their families. The fact that admission to a
nursing home comes at the end of a long series of disappoint-
ments undoubtedly negatively affects both the older individual and the family (Cath, 1972; Butler and Lewis, 1977; Fox
and Lithwick, 1978). York and Calsyn (1977) found that by
the time a family seeks to actually admit an aged relative to a
nursing home, the vast majority of families are no longer
willing to explore alternative options. Only 33 percent of their
respondents indicated that they would be willing to discuss
alternative living arrangements and supports for their older
relative at the time of admission. It appears that the introduction of alternative interventions once the family seeks to admit an aged relative is too late. The family has "reached the
end of their rope" and are no longer willing to consider other
options. These findings suggest that we need to begin to examine the factors that influence a family's propensity to consider institutionalization of an older person *before* the family
actually seeks this placement.

PURPOSE OF THE STUDY

This research investigated the planning by family members
for the institutionalization of their elderly relatives. As in

Teresi's (1980) study, institutional decision-making is conceptualized as a process construct, in that it encompasses the family's decision-making and planning while the aged relative still resides within the community. Drawn from the work of Janis and Mann (1977) on the decision-making process, institutional decision-making by the family for the older person is conceptualized as having four stages: *recognition* of the potential for institutionalization; *discussion* of the institutionalization option; *implementation* of action steps towards institutionalization; and *placement* of the relative in the institutional setting.

This research is a prospective study which focuses on the first three stages of institutional decision-making. The research question is: What are the most salient structural and dynamic factors associated with each stage of the institutional decision-making, and do these critical factors vary with each stage of the institutional planning process?

METHODS

Findings reported here stem from a larger study that investigated the consequences for families of terminating state-funded chore services for elderly. Data were collected through interviews with 80 families of both terminated (42) and continued (38) elderly chore clients. Structured interviews, averaging 45 minutes in length, were conducted in respondents' homes and elicited information concerning caregiving behaviors, burden, plans for institutional care, and demographic data.

The sample consisted of family members in four targeted western Washington counties who: (1) considered themselves the primary person providing assistance to their older relative, (2) lived within a one hour's driving distance of their relative, and (3) were willing to be interviewed. The demographic characteristics of the sample are presented in Table 1. The majority of caregivers were adult children including daughters (44%), sons (27%), and daughters-in-law (5%). The sample was predominantly caucasian (89%) and married (71%). The caregiver's median age was 56 and median family income was $20,000. The majority of caregivers (55%) were employed either full-time (30%) or part-time (13%).

Table 1

Demographic Characteristics

of Caregivers

	n	%
SEX		
Male	21	26.2
Female	59	73.7
RELATIONSHIP TO ELDER		
Spouse	1	1.2
Child	60	75.0
Sibling	8	10.0
Niece/Nephew	4	5.0
Other Relative	7	8.7
MARITAL STATUS		
Married	57	71.2
Not Married	23	28.8
EMPLOYMENT STATUS		
Full-time	36	45.0
Part-time	13	16.2
Not Employed	31	38.7
AGE (MEDIAN)	56.0	
FAMILY INCOME (MEDIAN)	20,000	

MEASURES

Drawing from Horowitz's (1982) study of predictors of family caregiving involvement, two sets of independent variables, structural and dynamic variables, are examined in this study. The structural factors studied fall into three categories: elder characteristics (gender, living arrangement, and functional ability); caregiver characteristics (gender, age, kinship relation to elder, and marital, health and employment status); and family characteristics (income, assistance and responsibility). The dynamic factors examined fall into two categories: caregiving involvement (personal care, household, community and psychosocial assistance and time commitment); and perceptions of the caring role (burden, stress, affection and familial obligation). Table 2 presents information on the measurement of these independent variables. The first three stages of institutional decision-making, the dependent variables, are operationalized in the following manner:

Table 2

Measures of Independent Variables

	VARIABLE	MEASURE
Structural Variables		
Elder Characteristics	Gender	Male; Female
	Living Arrangement	Alone; With spouse; With others
	Activities of Daily Living (ADL)	Modification of the OARS Multidimensional Functional Assessment Questionnaire. Asked whether elder could accomplish 15 tasks without any help, with some help or completely unable to do it without assistance.
Caregiver Characteristics	Gender	Male; Female
	Age	Years of age
	Kinship Relation to Elder	Husband; Wife; Son; Daughter; Son-in-law; Daughter-in-law; Sister; Brother; Grandchild; Nephew; Niece and Other Relative
	Marital Status	Married; Not-Married
	Health Status	Perfect; Very good; Good; Fair; Poor
	Employment Status	Not employed; Employed part-time; Employed full-time
Family Characteristics	Income	Average annual household income before taxes and deductions
	Assistance	Number of family members, in addition to primary caregiver, providing some support for elder

Table 2 continued

	Responsibility	Number of family members, in addition to elder, the primary caregiver is responsible for and assists
Dynamic Variables		
Caregiving Involvement	Personal Care Assistance	10-item scale assessing caregiving support with feeding; bathing; dressing; toileting; appearance; medications; nursing care; bed transfer; wheelchair transfer; and walking
	Household Assistance	5-item scale assessing caregiver support with yard care; laundry; meal preparation; housework; and telephone assistance
	Community Assistance	4-item scale assessing caregiver support with transportation; shopping and errands; handling money, and personal business
	Psychosocial Assistance	2-item scale assessing caregiver support with telephone check-up and companionship
	Time Commitment	Total amount of time committed by the caregiver in all support activities for elder in month preceding interview
Perceptions of Caring Role	Perceived Burden	Modification of Zarit (1981) Burden Scale. A 5-point, 11-item inventory tapping the impact of the caring role on such aspects as personal freedom, privacy, time to one's self, and relationships with family and friends
	Perceived Stress	A single global question asking respondents to rate on a 5-point scale the amount of stress they are feeling in relation to caring for their older relative

Table 2 continued

Perceived Affection

A 5-point, 13-item inventory assessing the
degree to which the caregiver had positive
feelings toward the elder and perceives their
relationship as positive and enjoyable.
Respondents are asked to rate how often they
experienced such feelings as guilt, pleasure,
depression, and manipulation

Familial Obligation

Taps the extent to which the respondent feels
a sense of duty to care for older relative.
Subjects place an X on a 10-point scale with 1
representing the government as totally
responsible; 5, government and families
equally responsible, and 10, families are
totally responsible

Stage 1: Recognition

Family caregivers were asked, "During the past year, have you ever thought about placing your (relative) in a nursing home, a home for the aged, or some other type of institution in five circumstances: given her/his present condition; if s/he required constant care; if s/he becomes incontinent; if s/he becomes senile; or if her/his condition worsens in any other way." Respondents were asked to rate each item in terms of having given either: no consideration; slight consideration; moderate consideration; or great consideration. Recognition of the institutional option, thus, is measured by summing across this five-item inventory.

Stage 2: Discussion

Family caregivers were asked, "During the past year have you discussed the possibility of placing your (relative) in a nursing home or other type of institution with any of the following persons: family members; friends; doctors; nurses; social workers; psychologists; physical therapists; nurse's aides; clergy; and others. Responses were recorded as either yes or no, and summed across items. The family caregiver's discussion of institutionalization score, thus, represents the total number of types of persons the caregiver spoke to about this issue.

Stage 3: Implementation

Family caregivers were asked, "Have your concerns about your (relative) prompted you to take any of the following actions in the past year: requested the names of specific nursing homes or institutions from family, friends or professionals; contacted or visited any nursing home or institution's facilities with an interest of learning how they might suit your (relative's) needs; obtained the admissions applications for any institution; submitted an admissions application to any institution; or placed your (relative's) name on a waiting list for a particular institution." Responses were recorded as either yes or no and summed across these five items.

Correlational analysis was performed to examine the

strength of the interrelationship between these three identified stages of institutional decision-making. As Table 3 shows, each stage correlates strongly (p .001) with the other two stages.

LIMITATIONS OF THE STUDY

While the conceptual approach taken in this study presumes that institutionalization is a decision-making process that evolves as a series of steps or stages over a period of time, the data utilized in this study are derived from a cross-sectional study. In cross-sectional research cause can not be inferred. Also, the data were collected from a relatively small purposive sample of primary family caregivers of current or terminated chore services clients. Reflecting the chore services population, the sample is predominantly white. Moreover, while the family caregivers represent a wide range of socioeconomic levels, the dependent older persons have limited economic means.

RESULTS

Correlates of Institutional Decision-Making

The data were first analyzed using Pearson product moment correlations. Correlational coefficients were computed for the three stages of institutional decision-making and the independent variables (see Table 3). Bivariate analysis revealed both commonalities and differences in the factors correlated with each state of institutional planning. Four structural variables were found to be correlated with all three stages: the elder's living arrangement; the elder's ADL functioning status; the kinship relation between caregiver and receiver; and family income. Caregivers of older relatives having greater impairment in their abilities to perform the activities of daily living (ADL) and living in the homes of other family members were more likely to have engaged in institutional planning. The more distant the kinship bond between caregiver and receiver (i.e., niece, nephew, or grandchild rather than spouse, daughter or son), the more likely institutional decision-making.

Table 3

Zero-Order Correlations of the Stages of

Institutional Decision-making with Selected Variables

	Stage 1 Recognition	Stage 2 Discussion	Stage 3 Implementation
Stage 1 Recognition	----	.65***	.49***
Stage 2 Discussion	.65***	----	.64***
Stage 3 Implementation	.49***	.64***	----
STRUCTURAL VARIABLES			
Elder's Living Arrangement	.27**	.38**	.28**
Elder's ADL Impairment	-.22*	-.29*	-.22*
Caregiver's Gender	-.15	-.17	-.20*
Kinship Relationship	.22*	.27*	.24*
Caregiver's Health Status	-.11	-.17	-.20*
Caregiver's Employment Status	.29**	.18	.06
Family Income	.43***	.21*	.20*
Family Responsibility	.20*	.24*	.17
DYNAMIC VARIABLES			
Personal Care Assistance	.33***	.47***	.43***
Household Assistance	.13	.20*	.12
Community Assistance	.26*	.25*	.10
Perceived Burden	.25*	.29**	.18
Perceived Stress	.34***	.25*	.19*
Perceived Affection	.43***	.26*	.19*
Familial Obligation	-.09	-.11	.02

*p .05   **p .01   ***p .001

Families with greater financial resources were more likely to engage in institutional planning.

Structural variables found not to be correlated with any of the stages were: the elder's gender; the caregiver's age; and the caregiver's marital status. The caregiver's employment status was correlated with only stage 1. Employed caregivers gave greater consideration to the potential institutionalization of their older relative than those caregivers who were not employed. Family responsibility was correlated with stages 1 and 2, but not with stage 3. Caregivers who were assisting or were responsible for a larger number of family members more often considered and discussed placing their older relative in a nursing home. Conversely, the caregiver's gender and health status were correlated with stage 3, but not stages 1 and 2. Male caregivers and caregivers with poor health were more likely to act on institutionalization.

Three dynamic variables were found to be significantly associated with all three stages of institutional planning: personal care assistance; stress; and affection. Family caregivers who assisted their older relatives with personal care tasks such as feeding, bathing and dressing were more likely to consider, discuss and act on institutionalization. Also, caregivers who felt the present situation with their older relative had increased the amount of stress in their lives were more likely to engage in institutional planning. Finally, the more positively the caregiver perceived the quality of their relationship with the elder, the less likely they would engage in institutional planning.

Three dynamic variables were found not to be correlated with any of the stages of institutional decision-making: the provision of psychosocial support; the time commitment; and perceptions of familial obligation. Both the perception of burden and provision of community assistance were significantly correlated with stages 1 and 2, but not stage 3. Caregivers who felt burdened by the caring role and provided community assistance were more likely to recognize and discuss institutionalization as an option.

Multivariate Analysis

The next step in the data analysis was to address the research question of what are the most salient predictors of a family's engagement in each stage of institutional decision-making. Given the exploratory nature of this study, stepwise regression analyses were used. Independent variables having a significant bivariate relationship with the dependent measures at the .05 level were selected as potential predictor variables. Table 4 presents the results of these multiple regressions on the three stages of institutional decision-making.

Forty three percent of the variance in the caregiver's recognition of the institutional option (stage 1) is explained by four variables. The affective relationship between the caregiver and receiver is the strongest predictor, accounting for 17 percent of the variance in reported behavior. When the affective relationship is controlled for, personal care tasks account for another 10 percent of the variance. Controlling for these two factors, three additional variables make significant contribu-

Table 4

Stepwise Multiple Regressions

of Stages of Institutional Decision-making

With Significant Variables

STAGE 1 RECOGNITION

	r	Beta	F
Perceived Affection	.41	.27	5.82
Personal Care Assistance	.35	.21	3.51
Family Income	.36	.30	7.48
Community Assistance	.31	.28	6.66
Elder's Living Arrangement	.22	.23	4.74

DF=5/63   R=.65 R^2=.43

STAGE 2 DISCUSSION

	r	Beta	F
Personal Care Assistance	.45	.38	13.17
Elder's Living Arrangement	.32	.28	7.09
Kinship Relationship	.32	.28	6.87

DF=3/63   R=.59 R^2=.35

STAGE 3 IMPLEMENTATION

	r	Beta	F
Personal Care Assistance	.42	.43	14.82
Caregiver's Gender	-.21	-.24	4.43

D=2/63   R=.48 R^2=.23

tions to explaining the variance in the consideration of institutionalization: family income (6%); community tasks (6%);
and elder's living arrangement (5%).

Thirty five percent of variance in the caregiver's engagement
in discussion of institutionalization (stage 2) is explained by
three variables. The strongest predictor is the performance of
personal care tasks accounting for 20 percent of the variance in
reported behavior. When personal care tasks are controlled
for, the elder's living arrangement accounts for another 7 percent of the variance. Controlling for these two factors, only
one other variable makes a significant contribution, the kinship
relationship, accounting for approximately 8 percent of the
variance.

Finally, twenty three percent of the variance in the caregiver's implementation of steps towards institutionalization

(stage 3) is explained by just two variables. Again, the strongest predictor is the performance of personal care tasks, accounting for approximately 18 percent of the variance in reported behavior. After controlling for personal care assistance, the caregiver's gender accounts for another 6 percent of the variance.

IMPLICATIONS OF FINDINGS

Cicirelli (1981) in his study of 164 adult children, found that while a majority of the children felt committed to providing intermediate levels of service to their parents, only a small minority were willing to assume the entire burden of services to parents. The data from this study support Cicirelli's findings. The findings suggest that as a family member progresses along the continuum of institutional decision-making the primary determinant becomes the objective level of caregiving involvement. Regression analyses revealed that while the primary predictor of the recognition of the option for institutionalization (stage 1) was the caregiver's perception of their affective relationship with the elder, the primary predictor of both the family member's discussion (stage 2) and implementation (stage 3) of steps toward institutional placement was the caregiver's performance of personal care tasks. Once family members are confronted with the need to perform personal care tasks for their older relatives, they begin to consider the transfer of responsibility and care from the family unit to the institution.

This relationship between the provision of personal care assistance and institutional decision-making may be a function of the family member's expectations and norms regarding their caregiving role. While family members may expect to assist their older relatives with managing their household, they may be unwilling or unable to provide personal care services. Assisting an older relative with intimate tasks may violate norms concerning appropriate family roles and interactions (Hooyman et al., 1985).

Another potential explanation for family member's reluctance to provide personal care assistance may lie in the nature of the delivery of these services. As noted by Horowitz (1982) and Montgomery et al. (1985), while family members may be able to schedule in two or three particular hours each week for errands, shopping, laundry, etc. for the older relative, personal care tasks often require a more intensive labor effort and are often performed in an on-call basis. The performance of many personal care tasks, such as toileting, bed or chair transfer and feeding, cannot be prescheduled, but rather must be flexible to respond to the immediate needs of the elder. Providing personal care help may, therefore, result in placing more constraints on, and greater disruption in the lives of family members.

An examination of the other predictor variables which contribute significantly to the explained variance in stages 2 and 3 after controlling for the performance of personal care tasks lend additional support to this interpretation that the strong relationship between personal care assistance and institutional decision-making may be in part a function of cultural expectations and norms. In the regression equation for stage 2, only the nature of the kinship relationship between caregiver and receiver adds significantly to the explained variance in the discussion of the institutional option. The more distant the kinship bond, the more likely the discussion of institutionalization. More distant family members are likely to feel less comfortable, willing, and/or obligated to perform intimate bodily tasks. In fact, the disabled older person may also feel this type of assistance is an inappropriate and unacceptable role for more distant family members.

In the regression model for stage 3, only one variable, the gender of caregivers, adds to explained variance in implementation of institutionalization steps. Male caregivers were more likely to engage in steps towards institutional placement than females. Again, cultural norms exist that women are the nurturers and provide the hands-on types of assistance to kin. The present cohort of older men may be ill-prepared to provide personal care assistance to disabled spouses or parents. Further, they may have been socialized to feel that performing these bodily tasks is inappropriate and, thus, are uncomfortable being thrust into this role.

These findings suggest that more distant relatives and/or male relatives may more quickly seek to institutionalize frail, older kin once personal care services are required. Conversely, closer kin and especially female relatives may be more willing to perform personal care tasks and, therefore, delay or prevent institutionalization of the disabled person. Social service and health professionals need to be made aware of these potential differences in caregiving involvement and institutional decision-making by gender and kinship bond. Male caregivers may need to be made more aware of formal supports within the community providing personal care assistance in order to keep the older person at home and prevent premature institutionalization. Horowitz (1985) found that although sons were less personally involved in the care of their aged parents than daughters, there were no differences between the sexes in the extent to which formal services were utilized by their older parents. Formal providers, thus, may not be stepping in to fill potential gaps in services. Women caregivers also need to be made aware of the existence of formal services within the community providing services for disabled or frail elders. The utilization of formal services as a supplement to their own caregiving role may prevent women from totally exhausting their own personal resources.

Simply making family caregivers aware of the existence of community services may not be enough. York and Calsyn (1977) found in their study of 76 families that although the majority of families know of alternative services, they did not utilize these services prior to seeking institutionalization of the older member. These findings suggest that social and health professionals must work with families to overcome their resistance to asking for help. An equally important question is even if families seek out these personal care services will they be able to purchase them? Currently personal care services are available only on a time-limited basis under Medicare benefits and are generally not funded through Medicaid.

It is interesting to note that caregiver's perceptions of familial obligation were not related to any of the stages of institutional planning. Respondents who indicated that families, rather than the government, should assume greater responsibility for the care of the aged were no more or less likely to engage in institutional planning. This finding suggests what people believe in the abstract may have little to do with their actions. This finding is further substantiated by Schorr's (1981) finding that when the question of filial responsibility is framed in simple and ethical terms most persons support the concept; however, these responses may be easily manipulated by introducing such issues as competing responsibilities for spouse or children, career advancement, etc.

This study's findings do differ from the findings of Teresi et al. (1980) concerning institutional risk. Teresi found that the caregiver's sense of being inconvenienced was the strongest predictor of elder's risk of institutionalization. This discrepancy in findings, however, may be in part an artifact of measurement. Teresi's (1980) scale of institutional risk includes items that require caregivers to make projections about their future actions concerning institutionalization. The present study, conversely, only asks caregivers to report past behaviors they have engaged in concerning institutional planning. Further, Teresi's (1980) measure of inconvenience asks caregivers not only the amount of inconvenience they experience in providing help to older person in specific activities of daily living, but also asks their willingness to perform these functions. Teresi's measure of inconvenience, thus, may be in fact tapping two separate constructs.

The findings of this study do support Horowitz's (1982) conclusion that both structural and dynamic factors are important to understanding family member's involvement and experience of caregiving. Structural and dynamic variables each make unique contributions to the prediction of the family caregiver's propensity to engage in the three stages of institutional decision-making. Thus, as Horowitz suggests, both sets of variables will need to be considered in the development of future research or interventive strategies.

REFERENCES

Brody, E.M. The aging family. *The Gerontologist,* 1966, 6, 202–206.
Butler, R.N., & Lewis, M. *Aging and Mental Health* (2nd Edition). St. Louis: The C.V. Mosby Publishing Company, 1977.
Cath, S.H. The institutionalization of a parent: A nadir of life. *Journal of Geriatric Psychiatry,* 1972, 5, 25–46.
Cicirelli, V.G. *Helping elderly parents: The role of adult children.* Boston: Auburn House, 1981.
Dobrof, R. *The care of the aged: A shared function.* Unpublished doctoral dissertation, Columbia University School of Social Work, 1976.

Fox, M., & Lithwick, M. Group work with adult children of confused institutionalized patients. *Journal of Long Term Care and Health Services Administration,* 1978, 121–131.

Hooyman, N.R., Gonyea, J.G. & Montgomery, R.J.V. The impact of un-home services termination of family caregivers. *The Gerontologist,* 1985, *25,* 141–145.

Horowitz, A. *Predictors of caregiving involvement among adult children of the frail elderly.* Paper presented at 34th Annual Meeting of the Gerontological Society of America, Boston, Massachusetts, November, 1982.

Horowitz, A. Sons and daughters as caregivers to older parents: Differences in role performances and consequences. *The Gerontologist,* 1985, *25,* 612–617.

Janis, I.L., & Mann, L. *Decision making: a psychological analysis of conflict, choice, and commitment.* New York: Free Press, 1977.

Kraus, A.S., Spasoff, R.A., Beattie, E.J., Holden, D.E.W., Lawson, J.S., Rodenburg, M., & Woodcock, G.M. Elderly application process: placement and care needs. *Journal of the American Geriatrics Society,* 1976, *24,* 165–172.

Lieberman, G.L. Children of the elderly as natural helpers: some demographic differences. *American Journal of Community Psychology,* 1978, *6,* 489–498.

Montgomery, R.J.V. & Borgatta, E.F. Family supports: a preventive approach. 1982 grant proposal (unpublished).

Montgomery, R.J.V., Gonyea, J.G. & Hooyman, N.R. Caregiving and the experience of subjective and objective burden. *Family Relations,* 1985, *34,* 19–26.

Schorr, A. " . . .*thy father & thy mother . . .", a second look at filial responsibility and family policy.* Washington, D.C.: United States Government Printing Office, 1980.

Teresi, J., Toner, J., Bennett, R., Wilder, D. *Factors Related to Family Attitudes Towards Institutionalizing Older Relatives.* Paper presented at 33rd Annual Meeting of the Gerontological Society of America, San Diego, California, November 1980.

U.S. Department of Health and Human Services, Health Care Financing Administration. *Long-Term care background and future directions.* Washington, D.C. U.S. Department Health and Human Services, 1981.

Vicente, L., Wiley, J.A., & Carrington, R.A. The risk of institutionalization before death. *The Gerontologist,* 1979, *19,* 361–367.

York, J.L., & Calsyn, R.J. Family involvement in nursing homes. *The Gerontologist,* 1977, *17,* 500–505.

Zarit, S.H., Reever, K.E., & Bach-Peterson, J. Relatives of the impaired elderly: correlates of feelings of burden. *The Gerontologist,* 1980, *20,* 649–655.

The Capacity to Care:
A Family Focused Approach
to Social Work Practice
With the Disabled Elderly

Stephen T. Moore, MSW, MPA

ABSTRACT. The social work profession has demonstrated a commitment to assisting the disabled elderly to maintain an independent life style within the community. The dual focus of the profession has led to the development of a variety of instrumental and psychosocial approaches to assist elders and their families. This paper addresses the conceptual basis for social work practice with elderly persons in non-institution settings. It involves a discussion of family caretaking process and an examination of the relevance of family theory to social work practice. A model is presented which would assist the practitioner in integrating instrumental and psychosocial approaches to serving the aged.

INTRODUCTION

The disabled elderly who live at home require social support to remain in the community. The family plays a central role in the system of social support. As a result, for other sources of support to be effective, they must be integrated to complement the families' efforts. Social workers make an important contribution to this process by properly integrating family and community support systems.

It is a well known "social" fact that the elderly are a grow-

Stephen T. Moore is a doctoral student at the University of Kansas School of Social Welfare. The author wishes to thank Donald Chambers, PhD, James Taylor, PhD, and Ann Wieck, PhD, for their assistance in the preparation of this manuscript.

ing segment of American society. Since 1900, the number of persons 75 years of age and older has increased ten-fold, and the number of persons over 85 years of age has increased seventeen-fold (Treas, 1979). The vast majority (95 percent) of those over 65 remain in the community (Shanas, 1979b). Shanas (1979b) reports that 17 percent of these elderly experience limited mobility due to a chronic condition, and 5 percent are classified as homebound. These are the elderly who most require the integrated services of family and formal support systems.

This paper discusses the role of social work practice in the community-based long-term care system (home care). It examines the nature of family caretaking and the fit between family and formal sources of care. A case is made for a family-focused case management approach which integrates instrumental and psychosocial interventions. The discussion concludes with a presentation of a conceptual practice model that addresses both situational and relationship factors in the caretaking process.

Home-delivered health and social services have recently received widespread acclaim as an option in caring for the frail elderly. This is because such services are thought to reduce costs and maximize values important to society. However, the concept of providing care to the elderly in their homes is not new. Families, tribes, and other social units have been providing such services for centuries (Beauvoir, 1972). The nature of the care given to the elderly has reflected religious and cultural values of society and its economic resources. Only in contemporary times have specialized institutions, such as home health agencies, been developed to complement the efforts of family support.

The home-care system is a complex network of health and social agencies which assist families in caring for the frail elderly (S. Brody, 1973). The coordination of such a variety of services leads to both pragmatic and conceptual dilemmas. This discussion focuses on the conceptual problems related to the integration of family and formal caring systems. This analysis is undertaken from a social work frame of reference. That is, it attempts to organize ideas in a way that captures the complexity of person and environment transactions.

FAMILY PROVISION OF CARE

The family is the primary support system for the frail elderly. More than any other institution, it provides for the physical and emotional well-being of the aged (S. Brody et al., 1978). It has been estimated that the family provides 80 percent of all home care services (National Center for Health Statistics, 1972). Without adequate family support, the cost of maintaining the frail elderly at home exceeds that of institutional care (General Accounting Office, 1977a, 1977b).

This section reviews the status of the family as a giving institution in terms of its past, present, and anticipated performance. It also examines the fit between family structure and the service delivery system.

Historical evidence exists which calls into question the quality of life experienced by the elderly of past generations. As Simone de Beauvoir (1972) graphically illustrates, some primitive societies were nothing less than brutal in their treatment of the nonproductive elderly. Maryl (1982) points out that the preindustrial family, which is often the object of romantic nostalgia, was not burdened with expectations regarding marital bliss and personal fulfillment, as is today's family. The stability of preindustrial families does not necessarily reflect the level of emotional fulfillment that current interpretations may be tempted to assign to it.

Romantic conceptions of preindustrial family life tend to neglect two important factors. First, since the life span was shorter, the probability of living to old age was lower. Thus the burden of care for the elderly was not so great. Second, in earlier times, families were a primary economic institution. Wealth was concentrated in the hands of the oldest members. Therefore, the role of the elderly reflected their higher economic status (Maryl, 1982).

The demystification of past family relationships affords us a more rational ground for dealing with family problems of today. The nucleation of modern families has provided considerable benefits, both to individuals seeking self fulfillment and to society which demands a specialized and mobile work force. The transfer of family functions to the larger society has resulted in the more effective performance of those functions. Few would contend that families are capable of the level of performance demonstrated by modern educational, medical, or manufacturing institutions. The cost of these achievements has been the role displacement of the elderly in family life. However, despite the effect of social change on the role of the elderly, the family remains a vital caring system.

Research documents that families are actively involved with their elders. The notion that the elderly are isolated from their families is clearly a myth (Shanas, 1979a). Of those 65 years of age or older, eighty-nine percent of the men and 59 percent of the women have a live-in partner or spouse (U.S. Bureau of the Census, 1975). A review of the research shows that 80 percent of the elderly have living children and 75 percent of this group either live in the same household or within a thirty minute drive of at least one child (Butler & Lewis, 1982). The frequency with which children visit their parent(s) has not changed dramatically over the past twenty years (Shanas, 1979a). Of the elderly who had children in 1955, 83 percent had seen at least one child in the week prior to the interview. In 1975, this situation held true for 77 percent of the elderly interviewed.

The task of family caregiving tends to be focused on specific family members. In the face of sickness or impaired functional ability, the elderly turn first to their spouses and/or children (Kulys and Tobin, 1980; Shanas, 1979b). Wives and daughters tend to take on the caretaking role (Golodetz et al., 1969; Troll, 1971; Brody, 1981). This reflects our cultural expectations concerning gender-appropriate roles (Brody, 1981); the natural caretaking quality of such family relationships (Golodetz et al., 1969); and the fact that women tend to marry younger and live longer than men (Fengler & Goodrich, 1979).

The link between family care and the ability to stay at home is well established. Family support is essential if institutionalization of the elderly is to be avoided. Research indicates that nursing home residents and home health care recipients do not differ significantly in terms of functional ability. The presence of a spouse or children was found to be the most significant variable in predicting the ability of the elderly to remain in their home for any given level of impairment (S. Brody et al.,

1978; Townsend, 1965). In fact, the elderly become more involved with their families as they become older and more frail (Johnson & Bursh, 1977). This is supported by reports that indicate elderly persons living alone are less infirm than those living with children, and the elderly who do not live near relatives are less infirm than those living with relatives (Johnson & Bursh, 1977). It is the 10 to 12 percent of the elderly who lack family resources who are most likely to be institutionalized or to require the services of social agencies (Puner, 1974). As the aging population grows, this will represent an increasing financial burden on the younger income earners.

Certain social trends give rise to concern about the future status of the family as a caring system. These trends include the following: (1) increased rates of divorce among the elderly (Uhlenberg & Myers, 1981); (2) increasing populations of the very old which put additional pressure on "young-old" caretakers (Treas, 1977; Block, 1982); (3) a decrease in multigenerational households (Mindel, 1979); and (4) the movement towards smaller family size which will place the caretaking burden on a fewer number of children (Treas, 1977). Troll cites that 40 percent of the elderly in the U.S. are great-grandparents. This reflects the emergence of the four-generation family, and brings into further question the future of the family as a caretaking institution.

Social change will require a rethinking of policy choices. The family, as the focus of public policy, brings to bear a fundamental political debate. It challenges our conception of what is public and what is private. Family focused policy evolves in the context of expectations regarding the nature of government responsibility (Kammerman & Kahn, 1978). The current political trend toward less government implies that the family must do more (Steiner, 1981; Frankfather et al., 1981). The family, according to Steiner (1981), is considered "the last bastion of privacy in an already overregulated world" (p. 9).

On the other hand, support to families is justified in terms of maximizing freedom and choice (Frankfather et al., 1981). Obviously, the provision of home care to families increases the options available to them. This position is strengthened by the argument that systemic social forces have impaired the family's ability to support its elderly. The case can be made that the changes in family structure that diminished the support available to the elderly were necessitated by the demands of an industrial society. The notion of social causation supports the case for social responsibility.

Once the case of social responsibility is established, the economy and humanity of the family make it an attractive alternative in caring for the frail elderly (Shanas & Sussman, 1982; Steiner, 1981; Kammerman & Kahn, 1978). A primary policy objective becomes balancing familial and societal responsibility. This requires a conceptual framework which relates family structure and functioning to a service delivery system which supports desirable characteristics and minimizes unwanted consequences.

Litwak (1965) puts forth such a framework. He suggests that there exists four basic types of family structures: (1) the extended family; (2) the dissolving family; (3) the isolated nuclear family; and (4) the modified extended family. He further suggests that there are three ways in which service delivery systems tend to interact with families in caring for the elderly. The service delivery system may substitute for, complement, or compete with the efforts of families. The type of relationships between the delivery system and the family depends in part on the structure of the family (Litwak, 1965; Nelson, 1982). For example, services to the elderly in a nuclear, isolated family may substitute for the family support whereas, in a modified extended family, services tend to complement the efforts of the family. In a tightly-closed, extended family system, services could likely compete with the efforts of the family.

Critics have expressed concern that the provision of services to the elderly in their homes may compete with family caretaking and lead family members to do less. They contend that public support may undermine the strength and solidarity of the family unit. However, a recent study indicates (Frankfather et al., 1981) that families do not dramatically reduce the amount of services they provide for their elders when formal supports are made available. In cases where family support was reduced, it was in response to a realistic physical limitation on the part of an equally frail caregiver.

The dilemma of integrating formal services with family care brings to bear a critical practice question. Litwak (1965) and others (Nelson, 1982; Shanas & Sussman, 1981) have suggested that the optimal match of family structure and service delivery system is a modified extended family where services are delivered that complement those provided by the family. This situation assures adequate care of the elderly, without creating either undue burden for the family or prohibitive cost to society.

Litwack (1965) contends that the modified extended family is the dominant structure in modern society. This contention is supported by the vast array of empirical studies reviewed in this discussion. These studies clearly demonstrate the involvement of elders with their families. As Shanas and Sussman (1981) point out, the modern family is a complex network of individuals related by marriage or blood. They write:

> For most older people, the family is that group of individuals to whom they are related by blood or marriage. It includes more than spouse, children, and siblings. The family includes cousins of various degrees, in laws, and a variety of relatives who enter the family network as a need for service, help or information arises. (p. 213)

The actualization of a social work practice based on ecological principles has not been achieved. Development in this area requires new conceptual tools. The fit between family structure and the service delivery system forms the context of practice. If social work practice is to address both coping behaviors and environmental issues, an integrative model must be developed. The following section examines the evolution of family theory and presents a model for integrating family dynamics and environmental concerns.

IMPLICATIONS FOR PRACTICE

The overall goal of social work practice is to enhance the match between individuals and their environment. Case management is a social work practice model which addresses both coping behaviors and environmental concerns. The function of case management is to evaluate needs and subsequently to monitor and coordinate services (General Accounting Office, 1979). It involves a variety of casework skills including assessment, brokering, enabling coordinating, monitoring, and evaluating (Bertsche and Horeisi, 1980; Intagliata, 1980; Sullivan, 1981). When conceptualized within a social work frame of reference, this model of practice is expanded to include clinical activities that assist families in mobilizing their personal resources to meet the demands of caring (Bertsche and Horeisi, 1980). The skilled case manager is a generalist who works well at both the individual and systems level (Sussman, 1982; Scanlon et al., 1979).

The nature of practice with families caring for the elderly is determined, largely, by the way in which we conceptualize intergenerational transactions. The psychoanalytic model has impeded the development of a clinical theory of the family which views family caretaking across generations outside of the narrow constructs of role-reversal and dependency (Goldfarb, 1965; Block, 1982). Recently, the concept of filial responsibility has emerged in the literature. It describes the developmental nature of the process by which adult offspring assume caretaking responsibility for their aging parents (Block, 1982; Seelbach, 1984).

The concept of filial responsibility was described by Shorr (1960) in terms of the obligations of an adult child to meet the needs of their parents. Blenkner (1965) offers a richer conception of this process. She describes a process in which the parent-child relationship evolves into a reciprocal relationship between two adults, where the rights, limitations and needs of both individuals are both respected (Blenkner, 1965; Block, 1982). The evolution of "parent-child" relationships into "person-to-person" relationships is considered the hallmark of healthy family functioning (Bowen, 1977).

Family system theory represents a movement away from individual psychopathology toward concepts that capture the interactional nature of family process. These concepts include family loyalties (Boszormeny-Nagi & Spark, 1973), family structure (Minnuchin, 1974; Miller, 1981), and the family life cycle (Carter & McGoldrick, 1980; Williamson, 1981). The evolution of family theory made a significant contribution to our understanding of family caregiving.

However, traditional family system theories tend to neglect environmental factors. Social ecology asserts that "human behavior cannot be understood apart from the environmental context in which it occurs" (Moos, 1974; p. 21). It is concerned with both human adaption and social milieu. Models of family functioning which portray this contextual dimension are beginning to emerge. Olson and McCubbin (1983) emphasize that family stress may be precipitated by predictable (normative) events associated with the family life cycle and by unpredictable events (non-normative) which are imposed upon the family by the larger environment. They contend that family coping should be conceptualized as the behaviors, cognitions, and perceptions of family members while contending with stressful life events.

Social work has a historical commitment toward mitigating the stress of family living. Early work concentrated on destructive environmental forces (Richmond, 1917). This was followed by a trend towards psychodynamic interpretations of family life (Burgess, 1926). Social work practice has also been heavily influenced by the family therapy movement. Recent attempts have been made to expand this model to include nontraditional living arrangements as legitimate family structures and to account for the dynamic interplay between family process and the large social environment (Hartman, 1981).

A comprehensive theoretical structure which completely describes the dynamics of person and environment transactions does not exist. If practice is to be knowledge guided, practitioners must find a way of integrating various theoretical explanations in a meaningful way (Chambers, 1975). This requires the development of a frame of reference which organizes various theories into a functional guide, and which captures the interactional nature of social life (Bartlett, 1975).

The home-care arena requires a special emphasis on the social ecology of the caregiving process. In its various forms, the family is the built-in environment of the frail elderly (Sussman, 1972). An attempt to model the dynamics of the family caregiving process will be offered in this section. As a model, it is not so specific as to be considered a theory, nor is it so broad as to be considered a frame of reference. Rather, it is presented as a tool for integrating various theoretical perspectives within a social work frame of reference.

The model presented here delineates the stress incurred by families as emanating from both intra-family relationships (relationship stress) and by stressors with the larger environment (situational stress). The model demonstrates that family caregiving may contribute to the family's well being up to the threshold point at which situational and/or relationship factors cause disharmony with the family system. The ability of a family to care for its frail elderly depends then on a host of relationship and situational factors. In an attempt to model the various factors involved in the family caregiving process, the following assumptions are presented.

—Family caretaking can contribute to the emotional integration of the entire family unit (Bowen, 1977).
—It is often emotional, not physical, barriers which cause the greatest burden in the caretaking process (Bowen, 1977).
—Each family member has a threshold of caretaking that can be provided beyond which dysfunction response patterns emerge (Frankfather et al., 1981).
—The ability of a family to provide care for its elderly depends, in part, on situational factors: the environmental demands upon and resources of the family (Hartman, 1981).

An attempt is made here to construct a schematic model of stress and the well being of families involved in the caretaking process. The task, then, becomes one of illustrating the relationship among the following variables: (1) the level of relationship stress; (2) the level of situational stress; (3) the level of care-taking provided by a family; and (4) the level of well being of a family. This model demonstrates the concept that, for a given family, a threshold of well-being exists. Up to this threshold point, the provision of care should contribute to the emotional well being of the family. When family resources are pushed beyond their personal, physical, and financial capabilities the well-being of the family deteriorates. These relationships are conceptualized as a capacity to care curve (Fig. 1).

The capacity-to-care curve is a conceptual tool, in that it conceptualizes the relationship of various factors for a family with a given set of characteristics. Its usefulness as a concept for guiding policy and practice lies in its ability to simplify a complex set of relationships. The capacity to care curve suggests that social workers who function as casemanagers in home care should address both situational (environmental)

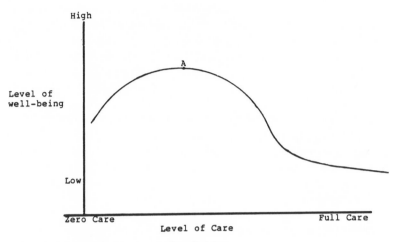

Figure 1
Capacity-to-Care Curve

A = Capacity to care threshold

and relationship factors. The social worker arranges an integrated service package which combines instrumental services (e.g., home making) and psychological service (e.g., family counseling) so that the efforts of families are complemented and their caring capacity is maximized.

The following is a presentation of two case studies. In the first example, the process by which an elderly individual's requirements for care eclipse the caregiving capability of the family is portrayed. This case study illustrates that institutional placement is often sought when the caregiver is overwhelmed by the need of the elderly family member. The second case study demonstrates how social work case management integrates instrumental and psychosocial approaches. This case study illustrates how an integrated approach can mitigate both the physical and emotional burden of caregiving.

CASE STUDY #1

Mr. and Mrs. Smith celebrated their golden anniversary 3 years ago. They reside in a comfortable ranch style home in a suburb of a large city in the Midwest. Mr. Smith retired from his job as a personnel director 14 years ago at the age of 63.

Mrs. Smith, a school teacher and 2 years Mr. Smith's junior retired one year later. The Smiths have two children, a daughter and a son. The daughter, who is the oldest, lives in the same town. She is married, has three teenage children and has a part time private law practice. The son who is in his thirties has never married, and lives on the west coast where he is part owner of a restaurant.

Mr. and Mrs. Smith have some common interests and have always enjoyed traveling together. However, they have also enjoyed many interests quite separate from each other. During the first years of retirement, though they did travel abroad and play tennis together regularly, each partner put most of his or her energy into separate interests. Mr. Smith took frequent hunting and fishing trips while Mrs. Smith started a small art gallery as a joint venture with a long-time friend.

Five years ago, two events drastically altered this couple's idyllic retirement life style. First, Mr. Smith suffered a severe stroke and was left paralyzed completely on one side. Mrs. Smith put aside her gallery in order to assist in her husband's recovery. She assisted with the treatment plan developed by the visiting nurse and physical therapist. Her business partner and long-time friend visited her daily to provide support and kept her in touch with the art community. The Smith's daughter also kept in constant touch during this time.

The second event was more traumatic for Mrs. Smith than the first. Six months after her husband's stroke, her best friend and business partner was killed in a car accident. That same week she was told that her husband had reached his full rehabilitation potential and that his aphasia was not expected to improve. For the first time in Mrs. Smith's life, she felt trapped, cut off from the outside world, living with a spouse she loved but could not communicate with.

Mrs. Smith had always been a creative and energetic in her personal and professional pursuits. However, she tended to rely on others in legal and financial matters. When Mrs. Smith's husband became disabled, her daughter took over managing the family's affairs. Mrs. Smith appreciated this help, but often resented the manner in which her daughter made decisions without consulting her. When Mrs. Smith's business partner was killed, Mrs. Smith reluctantly conceded to her daughter's insistence that the business be sold.

For the last five years, Mrs. Smith has lived alone with her husband. He spends most of his day watching sports on television or pondering through fishing magazines. She believes that he could walk with a walker, but he insists on using a wheel chair. His speech is slurred and his moods often swing from anger to depression.

The couple's son visits once every 12 to 18 months, but their daughter visits twice a week, Tuesday and Friday. On Tuesday she has lunch and then visits about an hour. She brings with her any items that Mrs. Smith might request. On Fridays, Mrs. Smith goes out shopping and to a pottery class while her daughter stays with Mr. Smith. Mrs. Smith claims these weekly outings keep her from going "crazy."

When her daughter revealed that she had accepted an offer to become a senior partner in a firm, located in a city 75 miles away, Mrs. Smith was shocked. Determined to keep active, she decided to take her husband to a daycare center on Fridays while she shopped and continued her pottery class. She informed her husband of this and his acceptance was coupled with depression. On the first day, as Mrs. Smith attempted to transfer her husband into the car, they both fell onto the driveway. Mrs. Smith was able to get up and call an ambulance while Mr. Smith agonized on the ground.

Mr. Smith was kept in the hospital while Mrs. Smith was treated and released. The hospital social worker informed Mrs. Smith that her husband has a broken hip and that with his paralysis the recovery period will be very difficult. After examining the family's situation, the social worker asked Mrs. Smith to consider whether she would prefer to have her husband go home or whether she would consider placing him.

During the next two weeks, this decision weighed heavily on Mrs. Smith's mind. Her husband became increasingly depressed and his speech more confused. Her daughter visited at the hospital only on Sundays and her son had called only once. Finally, two days before her husband was released, Mrs. Smith called her daughter and explained that the next day she would tell her husband that following hospitalization he must go to a nursing home. Mrs. Smith also informed her daughter that she was going to spend a month in New York with a cousin to recover from this horrible ordeal.

CASE STUDY #2

Two elderly sisters, Mrs. Jones and Ms. Adams, have lived together for approximately ten years. The younger, Mrs. Jones, is widowed and has lived with her sister since the time of her husband's death. Mrs. Jones also has two married sons. One son lives out of town and the other lives only a few miles away. The son that lives close by helps with heavy chores such as putting in storm windows, but his wife and mother have always had a strained relationship. This limits the amount of time he can spend with his mother and precludes any assistance that the son's wife might provide.

The elderly sister, Ms. Adams, has never married. She ran a small business until she retired 15 years ago. Since that time she has been active in community and political affairs. At one time Ms. Adams had a strong friendship network; however, in recent years a number of her friends have died or moved closer to their children.

Ms. Adams was warned by her doctor that she should slow down. Ms. Adams chose to ignore this advice, saying that community service and politics are what made life worth living. She claimed that she would rather risk a heart attack rather than become a "home body" like her younger sister. And that is exactly what happened. Ms. Adams suffered a serious heart attack and was released to the care of her younger sister after two weeks of hospitalization.

The relationship between these women has been one in which the older sister has functioned as the "over-responsible" independent, decision maker. The younger sister has always relied on the elder for guidance and direction. Since the stroke, the younger sister has been forced into making financial and other important decisions. She is confused and afraid; she is committed to keeping her sister at home but the relationship is strained.

In this case, home care includes a visiting nurse, a physical therapist, a home-health-aid and a homemaker all of which was arranged by the hospital social worker in coordination with the home-care social worker during the discharge planning process. Finances are adequate and the sisters have an informal helping network which provides assistance with shopping and transportation.

The home health social worker assists in coordinating these

various services so they fit the needs of the family. The worker also counsels with the sisters as they renegotiate their relationship. The younger sister is encouraged to become more independent and the worker gives the elder sister permission to be on the receiving side of the caregiving process. Gradually they form a new way of relating and experience capabilities within themselves previously untapped.

SUMMARY

The first case study simply illustrates that when the demands of family caregiving exceed a family's caring capacity, stress results. Family members are torn between their concern for their loved ones, their obligation to their immediate family and career responsibilities, and their personal well-being. Clearly, in this case continued family care would have resulted in the deterioration of the entire family unit.

In the second case, the family's capacity to care was maximized through the provision of a service package that integrated instrumental and psychosocial interventions. The effect of this intervention can be illustrated using the capacity-to-care curve. Prior to intervention, the family's threshold of caretaking was relatively low and the amount required exceeded their capabilities (see Figure 2). The lack of a good fit between the resources of the family and the demands of the situation would have resulted in a deterioration of the family's sense of well-being. Figure 3 illustrates that the psychosocial intervention resulted in maximizing the family's care-taking capacity. It also demonstrates that situational demands were mitigated through the application of instrumental services. The intervention served to enhance the family's coping skills and to change their environment. The family was not required to provide a level of care-taking which exceeded their capabilities. Formal services were integrated to complement the efforts of the family and other informal sources of care-taking.

The dual perspective of social work practice allows for the development of interventions that address both situational and relationship factors. The example illustrates how instrumental services and psychosocial intervention complement each other. Without the intervention of the homemaker (and

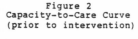

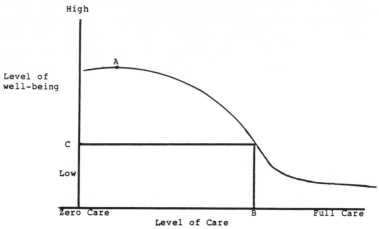

Figure 2
Capacity-to-Care Curve
(prior to intervention)

A = Capacity to care threshold
B = level of care required
C = level of well-being

other members of the home-care team), the stress generated by situational factors would have resulted in the deterioration of the well being of the family. Along with basic services, the sisters required assistance in renegotiating their relationship with each other. Clearly, an integrated approach is required to maximize the family's care-taking potential.

Social workers involved in the case management of home care services must use knowledge from a variety of sources in developing intervention strategies that fit the needs of the elderly. A person and environment frame of reference is necessary in order to achieve conceptual integration. The capacity-to-care curve is a model which attempts to reduce the complexity of this phenomenon so that meaningful practice acts may be formulated.

CONCLUSION

This paper has examined issues related to social work practice and family-focused case management in home care. The discussion began by establishing the family as the primary source of care for the homebound elderly. It then turned to an analysis of the conceptual underpinnings of the family care-taking process. A brief examination of family theory was presented; and the case was made for a conceptual model that would integrate concerns regarding family process with larger environmental issues. The capacity-to-care curve was offered as a model for guiding social work practice. This model conceptualizes stress as a phenomena that may be generated within families or that may be a product of environmental factors. Social work practice requires new conceptual tools which capture the complexity of person-environment transactions. The capacity-to-care curve is offered as a model which attempts to actualize the ecological principles which are "the common base of social work practice" (Bartlett, 1968).

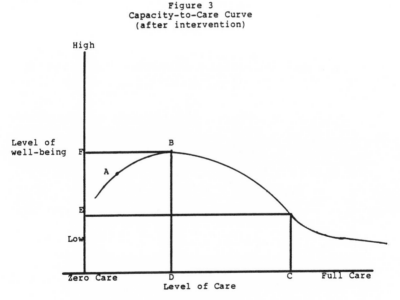

Figure 3
Capacity-to-Care Curve
(after intervention)

A = Capacity to care threshold
B = Capacity to care threshold after intervention
C = Level of care required of family prior to intervention
D = Level of care required after intervention
E = Level of well-being prior to intervention
F = Level of well-being after intervention

BIBLIOGRAPHY

Barlett, H. "The Place and Use of Knowledge in Social Work Practice." *Social Work*, 1964, *19*, 30–47.

Beauvoir, S. *The Coming of Age*. New York, Putnam and Sons, 1972.

Bertsche, A. and Horeisi, C. "Coordination of Client Services." *Social Work*, 1980, *25*, 94–98.

Blenkner, M. "Social Work and Family Relationships in Later Life." In E. Shannas & G. Strieb (eds.). *Social Structure and the Family: Gerontological Relations*. Englewood Cliffs, N.J.: Prentice-Hall, 1965.

Block, M. *The Role of Women Presented at the Commissioner's Forum of Aging, Intergenerational Relationships: The Role of the Family*. Paper presented at the *Commissioner's Forum on Aging*, "Intergenerational Relationships: The Role of the Family," Kansas City, MO, Oct. 7, 1982.

Boszormenyi-Nagi, I., and Spark, G. *Invisible Loyalities*. New York: Harper and Row, 1973.

Bowen, M. "A Systems View of the Aging Process." *The Georgetown Medical Bulletin*, 1977, *30*, 6–14.

Brody, E. "Women in the Middle and Family Help to Older People." *The Gerontologist*, 1981, *21*, 471–480.

Brody, S. "Comprehensive Health Care of the Elderly: An Analysis." *Gerontologist*, 1973, *13*, 412–418.

Burgess, E. "The Family as a Unity of Interacting Personalities." *The Family*, 1926, *7*, 3–7.

Butler, R., and Lewis, M. *Aging and Mental Health* (3rd ed.). C.V. Mosby, St. Louis, 1982.

Carter, E., and McGoldrick, M. *The Family Life Cycle: A Framework for Family Therapy*. New York: Gardner Press, 1980.

Chambers, D. "Three Principles of a Knowledge-Guided Social Work Practice." *Journal of Social Welfare*, 1975, *2*, 35–43.

Frankfather, D., Smith, M., Caro, F. *Family Care of the Elderly: Public and Private Obligations*. Lexington Books, Lexington, 1981.

General Accounting Office. *Entering a Nursing Home—Costly Implications for Medicaid and the Elderly*. (Washington, D.C.: Government Printing Office, 1974).

General Accounting Office. *The Well-being of Older People in Cleveland, Ohio*. (Washington D.C.: Government Printing Office, 1977a).

General Accounting Office. *Home Health—The Need for a Policy to Better Provide for the Elderly*. (Washington, D.C.: Government Printing Office, 1977b).

Goldfarb, A. "Psychodynamics and the Three-Generation Family." In E. Shanas and G. Strieb (eds.). *Social Structure and the Family*. New York, Prentice-Hall, 1965.

Golodetz, A., Evans, R., Heinritz, G., and Gibson, C. "The Care of Chronic Illness: The 'Responsor's Role.' " *Medical Care*, 1969, *7*, 385–394.

Hartman, A. "The Family: A Central Focus for Practice." *Social Work*, 1981, *26*, 7–13.

Intagliata, J. "Promoting Human Services Integration Through Case Management." Paper presented at the *National Conference on Social Welfare,* July 30, 1980.

Kamerman, S. and Kahn, A. (eds.). *Family Policy: Government and Families in Fourteen Countries*. New York, Columbia University Press, 1978.

Kulys, R. and Tobin, S. "Older People and Their Responsible Other." *Social Work*, 1980, *25*, 138–145.

Litwak, E. "Extended Kin Relations in an Industrial Democratic Society." In E. Shanas and G. Striebs (eds.). *Social Structure and the Family*. New York, Prentice-Hall, 1965.

Maryl, W. "The Evolution of Intergenerational Support Paper Systems: A Comparison of Traditional and Modern Families." Paper presented at the *Commissioner's*

Forum on Aging, "Intergenerational Relationships: The Role of the Family," Kansas City, MO, Oct. 7, 1982.

Miller, J. "Family Support of the Elderly." *Family and Community Health: Aging and Health Promotion.* 1981, *13,* 39–49.

Mindel, C. "Multigenerational Family Households: Recent Trends and Implications for the Future." *Gerontologist,* 1979, *19,* 456–463.

Minuchin, S. *Families and Family Therapy.* Cambridge, Mass., Harvard University Press, 1974.

Moos, R. *Evaluating Treatment Environments: A Social Ecological Approach.* Wiley Books, New York, 1974.

National Center for Health Statistics. "The National Nursing Home Survey: 1972." *Summary for the United States, Vital and Health Statistics Series,* 13, No. 43, DHEW Publication No. PHS 79-1794.

Nelson, G. "Support for the Aged: Public and Private Responsibility." *Social Work,* 1982, *27,* 137–143.

Olson, D. and McCubbin, H. *Families: What Makes Them Work?* Sage Publications, Beverly Hills, 1983.

Puner, M. *"To the Good, Longer Life: What We Know About Growing Old.* Universal Books, New York, 1974.

Richmond, M. *Social Diagnosis.* Russell Sage Foundation, New York, 1917.

Schorr, A. "Filial Responsibility in the Modern American Family." (U.S. Dept. of Health Education and Welfare.) Washington, DC: U.S. Government Printing Office, 1960.

Shanas, E. "Social Myth as Hypothesis: The Case of Family Relations of Old People." *The Gerontologist,* 1979, *19,* 3–9(a).

Shanas, E. "The Family as a Social Support in Old Age." *The Gerontologist,* 1979, *19,* 169–174(b).

Shanas, E., Sussman, M. "The Family in Later Life: Social Structure and Social Policy." In James G. March (ed.). *Aging: Stability and Change in the Family,* New York: Academic Press, 1982.

Steiner, G. *The Futility of Family Policy.* The Booking Institution, Washington, D.C., 1981.

Sullivan, J. "Case Management." In John Talbott (ed.). *The Chronic Mentally Ill,* New York, Human Sciences Press, Inc., 1981.

Sussman, M. "Generational Linkages: Reciprocal Activities and Supports for Older and Younger Americans." Presented at the *Commissioners Forum on Aging,* "Intergenerational Relationships: The Role of the Family," Oct. 7, 1982.

Sussman, M. "A Policy Perspective on the United States Rehabilitation System." *Journal of Health and Social Behavior,* 1972, *13,* 152–161.

Townsend, R. "The Effect of Family Structure on the Likelihood of Admission to an Institution in Old Age." In E. Shanas and G. Striebs (eds.). *Social Structure and the Family.* New York: Prentice-Hall, 1965.

Treas, J. "Family Support Systems for the Aged: Social Demographic Considerations." *Gerontologist,* 1977, *17,* 486–491.

Troll, L. "The Family of Later Life: A Decade Review." *Journal of Marriage and Family,* 1971, *33,* 263–290.

Uhlenberg, P. and Myers, M. "Divorce and the Elderly." *Gerontologist,* 1981, *21,* 276–282.

U.S. Bureau of the Census. "Social and Economic Characteristics of the Older Populations." 1974. *Current Population Reports,* Series P-23, No. 57, Washington, D.C.: U.S. Government Printing Office, 1975.

Williamson, D. "Personal Authority Via Termination of the Intergenerational Hierarchical Boundary: A New Stage in the Family Life Cycle." *Journal of Marital and Family Therapy,* (Oct. 1), 1981, 50–57.

Burden, Coping and Health Status: A Comparison of Family Caregivers to Community Dwelling and Institutionalized Alzheimer's Patients

Clara Pratt, PhD
Scott Wright, EdM
Vicki Schmall, PhD

ABSTRACT. This study investigates caregiver health, burden and coping strategies of family caregivers to institutionalized and community-dwelling Alzheimer's disease patients. Patient residence was significantly related to caregiver health status, sources of burden and the efficacy of various strategies for reducing burden. Implications for intervention with family caregivers are discussed.

The objective difficulties and subjective sense of burden experienced by many family members who provide day-to-day care for physically and mentally impaired elders has been described by several authors (Zarit, Reever, and Bach-Peterson, 1980; Zarit and Zarit, 1982; Gwyther and Matteson, 1983; Archbold, 1983; Brody and Lang, 1983). In fact, institutionalization of dependent elders has been linked to these burdens becoming "excessive" (Tobin and Kulys, 1981; Carrilio and Eisenberg, 1983). Feelings of guilt and inadequacy often accompany institutionalization of a relative (Brody, 1977; Tobin

The authors are affiliated with Oregon State University, Corvallis, OR in the following capacities: Clara Pratt as Associate Professor, Human Development and Family Studies, and Director, Program on Gerontology, College of Home Economics; Scott Wright as a doctoral candidate, Human Development and Family Studies, College of Home Economics; and Vicki Schmall as Associate Professor, Human Development and Family Studies, and Gerontology Specialist.

and Kulys, 1981), but it is often assumed that institutionalization abates the stresses of caregiving. Smith and Bengston (1979), for example, note that institutionalization of a dependent relative may alleviate the strain of "technical care" and allow some families to refocus their efforts on the emotional aspects of their relationship.

While this may be true, little is known about the degree to which family caregivers whose relatives are institutionalized still define themselves as caregivers or still experience strains associated with this role. Further, little is known about how caregivers to either community dwelling or institutionalized elders cope with the strains of caregiving and the relationship of these coping efforts to caregiver's health and sense of burden. The current study investigates these questions, comparing family members who provide care for Alzheimer's patients at home and those who provide care in an institution.

METHOD

Instruments

Caregiver was defined as the person who had responsibilities for providing and/or supervising day to day care for the patient. The variables investigated in this study were caregiver burden, coping strategies, morale, self-assessed health before and after caregiving began and selected demographic factors (sex, age, patient residence, and length of caregiving). To gather data, three published documents and one investigator-designed instrument were utilized. The Caregiver Burden Scale (Zarit et al., 1981) consists of 22 items on feelings about caregiving and has a reported alpha reliability coefficient of .79 (Zarit, 1982). Each item is rated on a five point scale from zero (never) to four (nearly always). The caregiver burden score is the sum of all the responses and may range from zero to 88.

The Family Crisis Oriented Personal Evaluation Scales (F-COPES) consists of 30 items that represent eight coping strategies that individuals may use in response to problems or difficulties (McCubbin, Olsen and Larsen, 1981). While these strategies represent "only a small sampling of the expansive repertoire of coping responses actually used" (Olson and associates, 1983), the F-COPES does identify the frequency (from never [1] to very often [5]) of use of three internal and five external coping strategies. The three internal coping strategies are: Reframing (the ability to redefine stressful experiences in a way that makes them more understandable and manageable); Confidence in Problem-Solving; and Passivity (avoidance responses to problems) (McCubbin et al., 1983). The five external coping strategies reflect the degree to which individuals actually use the social support resources that may be available to them. These social resources include "Spiritual Support," "Extended Families," "Friends," "Neighbors," and "Community Services." The F-COPES has an alpha reliability of .86 and test/retest reliability of .81 (Olson et al., 1983).

Caregiver morale was measured using a seven item morale scale (Lawton, 1971) which assesses overall happiness and satisfaction with one's life. For example, specific items assessed satisfaction with life, the perception that life gets worse as one ages, and the level of unhappiness in one's current life. Scores range from 0 to 6.

A fourth instrument was utilized to gather descriptive information about the patient, and the caregivers. Some of the variables assessed were: the nature of caregiving responsibilities; hours per day spent caregiving; the patient's mental health status, place of residence, and length of illness; the caregiver's relationship to patient, health status, and the caregiver's perception of how caregiving had affected his/her health. An open ended question was also asked: "Is there anything else you would like to tell us to help us understand caregiving?"

Subjects

The subjects were caregivers to Alzheimer's patients and were drawn from two sources: ongoing support groups for Alzheimer's caregivers and one-time-only educational workshops or lectures on Alzheimer's Disease held at hospitals or senior centers. These support groups and most of the educational meetings were sponsored by local chapters of the Alzheimer's Disease and Related Disorders Association (ADRDA). It is possible that these subjects represent a biased sample, that is, caregivers who are seeking advice and support on management of relatives with Alzheimer's Disease.

Two-hundred and forty caregivers completed questionnaires. Because questionnaires were completed during the meeting times, the response rate was over 90% of those contacted. Sixty-one percent (146 respondents) were members of Alzheimer's support groups and 39% (94 respondents) were not. Initial analysis of all variables indicated no significant differences between respondents who were members of support groups compared to those who were not. Thus for all future analyses, data from these two sources were combined. The mean age of caregivers was 61.3 (sd = 14.6) and the mean length of caregiving was 49.1 months (sd = 14.7). Twenty-two percent (53 respondents) were male and 78 percent (187) were female. There were no significant differences in caregiver's mean age or mean length of caregiving by patient's residence. Sixty-two percent (149) of the caregivers provided care to relatives who resided in the community, either in the caregiver's home (50%) or their own home (12%). Twenty-eight percent (91) of the caregivers had relatives who resided in institutions.

Forty-four percent (106 respondents) were caregivers to husbands (patients' mean age = 72.9, and sd = 8.5), 14% (33 respondents) were caregivers to wives (patients' mean age = 72.6, sd = 6.2), and 42% (101 respondents) were caregivers to parents or parents-in-law (mothers, mean age = 77.5, sd = 9.8; fathers, mean age = 76.7, sd = 12.1; parents-in-law, mean age 74.3, sd = 12.4). There were no significant differences by patient residence in patients' mean ages or length of illness. However, compared to caregivers to community dwelling patients, caregivers to institutionalized patients were significantly more likely to rate the patient's mental status as poor (31.8% and 52.4%, respectively, Chi-square = 13.5, df = 3).

Procedures and Data Analysis

Questionnaires were distributed at the educational seminars on Alzheimer's Disease and Alzheimer's Caregivers support group meetings in urban and rural areas throughout a western state. Brief instructions were given and the researcher was available to answer questions and to assist respondents.

The cross-tabulation procedure of the Statistical Package for the Social Sciences (SPSS) was used to tabulate the date by frequency. Chi-square and Pearson correlation procedures were utilized to examine relationships between selected variables. Analysis of variance and t-test procedures were used to examine potential differences in coping strategies and burden scores by demographic and caregiving characteristics. Analysis of covariance was used to control for the effect of age when examining health as a variable. A significance level of .05 was established for all analyses.

FINDINGS

Caregiver Wellbeing: Burden and Health

The mean caregiver burden scores were 40.1 (sd = 17.5) for caregivers to community dwelling patients and 39.6 (sd = 18.7) for caregivers to institutionalized patients. There were no significant differences in burden scores by caregiver employment status, income level, use of service, patient residence, caregiver sex or family relationship (spouse, child, child-in-law) to the patient. Individual items with highest mean scores (Table 1) for caregivers to both community-dwelling and institutionalized elders are those that assessed the: perception that relative was dependent upon the caregiver (item #8); perception of the relative that only the family caregiver can provide care (item #14); fear of what the future holds for the relative (#7); and stress between caregiving and other responsibilities (#3).

Compared to caregivers to institutionalized patients, caregivers to community-dwelling patients gave significantly higher ratings to items that assessed lack of time for self (#2), negative impact of caregiving on their social life (#12) and relationships with friends (#6) and lack of privacy (#11). Community caregivers also gave significantly higher ratings to the feeling that their relative was dependent on them (#8). Caregivers to institutionalized patients gave significantly higher ratings to concerns about not having enough money to provide care (#15), being unable to continue providing care (#16), wishing they could leave the care to someone else (#18) and feeling they should do more (#20) (Table 1).

Table 1

Caregiver Burden Item[a] & Total Mean Scores by Patient
Residence (Total n=240)

How often** do you (caregiver) feel:	COMMUNITY DWELLERS (n=149)	INSTITUTIONAL DWELLERS (n=91)	t-value
1. your relative asks for more help than he/she needs	1.18 (sd=1.2)	.99 (sd=1.0)	1.31
2. you don't have enough time for yourself	2.21 (sd=1.2)	1.56 (sd=1.3)	4.27*
3. stressed between caregiving and other responsibilities	2.34 (sd=1.3)	2.25 (sd=1.4)	.58
4. embarrassed by relative's behavior	1.35 (sd=1.1)	1.22 (sd=1.2)	.98
5. feel angry around relative	1.34 (sd=1.0)	1.15 (sd=1.2)	1.45
6. your relative has a negative affect on relationship with friends and relatives	1.46 (sd=1.3)	1.17 (sd=1.3)	1.91*
7. afraid of the future for your relative	2.68 (sd=1.4)	2.69 (sd=1.4)	-.03
8. relative is dependent on you	3.48 (sd=1.0)	2.99 (sd=1.4)	3.10*
9. strained around relative	1.60 (sd=1.3)	1.79 (sd=1.4)	-1.14
10. your health has suffered by caregiving	1.59 (sd=1.2)	1.79 (sd=1.4)	-1.26
11. you do not have as much privacy as desired	1.96 (sd=1.5)	1.36 (sd=1.4)	3.29*
12. your social life has suffered	2.45 (sd=1.4)	1.99 (sd=1.5)	2.66*
13. uncomfortable having people over	1.47 (sd=1.4)	1.37 (sd=1.4)	.58
14. your relative expects that you are only one he/she could depend on	2.46 (sd=1.6)	2.13 (sd=1.6)	1.58
15. you don't have enough money to care	1.52 (sd=1.5)	2.09 (sd=1.6)	-2.97*
16. unable to care much longer	1.41 (sd=1.3)	1.89 (sd=1.6)	-2.34*
17. lost control of life	1.61 (sd=1.3)	1.88 (sd=1.5)	-1.55
18. wish you could leave care to someone else	1.29 (sd=1.3)	1.67 (sd=1.4)	-2.27*
19. uncertain about what to do for relative	1.85 (sd=1.3)	1.87 (sd=1.4)	-.27
20. you feel you should do more	1.61 (sd=1.2)	2.22 (sd=1.4)	-3.65*
21. could do better job caring	1.42 (sd=1.2)	1.42 (sd=1.3)	.03
22. Overall, how often do you feel burdened in caregiving	1.95 (sd=1.2)	1.90 (sd=1.3)	.14
TOTAL BURDEN (items 1-22)	40.1 (sd=17.5)	39.6 (sd=18.7)	-.09

[a]items are paraphrased
**scores range from 0=never, 1=rarely, 2=sometimes, 3=quite frequently, 4=nearly always
*$p \leq .05$

When the affect of age was controlled using analyses of co-variance, caregiver burden scores were significantly related to their health status for both caregivers to community patients [$F(3,135) = 10.7$] and institutionalized patients [$F(3,87) = 17.9$]. For both groups, burden scores were significantly higher for caregivers who rated their heath as fair or poor. Caregivers' ratings of their health status before caregiving began were not significantly related to the patients' residence, (Chi-square = 1.34, df = 3, Table 2). However, caregivers' ratings of their current health status were significantly related to patient residence (Chi-square = 9.60, df = 3, Table 2) with caregivers to institutionalized relatives significantly more likely to rate their current health status as "fair" or "poor." Caregivers to institutionalized relatives were also significantly more likely to state that caregiving had had a great negative affect upon their health status (Chi-square = 10.50, df = 2, Table 3).

Burden scores were not significantly related to length of caregiving for caregivers to institutionalized patients ($r = -.08$) or community dwelling patients ($r = -.04$), nor were burden scores significantly related to caregivers' age (community, $r = .01$; institutionalized, $r = -.11$) (Table 4).

Burden scores were significantly related to caregivers' morale levels for caregivers to community dwelling patients ($r =$

Table 2

Number and Percentage of Caregivers Reporting Levels of Health Status Before Caregiving and Currently, by Patient Residence

Patient Residence	Caregiver Health Status	
	Before Caregiving	Current (After Caregiving)[a]
Community n=149		
excellent	62(41.6%)	30(20.1%)
good	70(47.0%)	65(43.6%)
fair	13(8.9%)	41(27.5%)
poor	4(2.7%)	13(8.7%)
Institution n=91		
excellent	42(45.1%)	13(14.3%)
good	37(40.8%)	26(28.6%)
fair	10(10.9%)	36(39.6%)
poor	2(2.3%)	16(17.5%)
	$x^2=1.34, df=3, ns$	$x^2=9.60, df=3, p \leq .05$

[a]Caregivers to community-dwelling and institutionalized patients did not vary in age or length of caregiving.

Table 3

Number & Percentage of Caregivers Reporting Degree of Negative
Impact of Caregiving on Their Health, by Patient Residence (total n=240)

| | Impact of Caregiving on Health Status[a] | | |
	"A Great Deal"	"A Little"	"Not At All"
community-dwelling (n=149)	43(28.9%)	80(53.7%)	26(17.8%)
institutionalized (n=91)	43(47.2%)	32(35.2%)	16(17.5%)

[a]Comparing health before caregiving and health now, it was determined that in all cases, in which health status had changed, it was in the negative direction.
*x^2=10.50, df=2, p≤.01

$-.51$) and institutionalized patients (r = $-.49$) (Table 4). Morale scores did not vary significantly by caregiver sex (males mean 3.2, sd = 2.1; females mean = 3.2, sd = 1.8; t = .69, df = 238) or patient residence (community, mean = 3.2, sd = 1.8; institution mean = 3.00, sd = 1.9; t = .36, df = 238).

Caregiver Coping Strategies

Coping strategies used by caregivers did not vary significantly by caregiver sex or patient residence. Among the internal coping strategies, Reframing was the highest rated (mean = 3.86, sd = .72) followed by Confidence in Problem-Solving (mean = 3.59, sd = .84) and Passivity (mean = 2.21, sd = .75). For the external coping strategies, Community Services were rated the highest (mean = 3.72, sd = .93) followed by: Friends (3.59, sd = .85); Spiritual Support (3.53, sd = 1.15); Extended Family (3.47, sd = .99); and Neighbors (2.59, sd = 1.03).

Despite the lack of differences by patient residence in use of the various coping strategies, relationships between caregiver burden scores and use of various strategies did vary by patient residence. For caregivers to community dwelling relatives, burden scores were significantly correlated with passivity (r = .28), spiritual support (r = $-.26$) and the extended family (r = $-.18$). For caregivers to institutionalized relatives, burden was significantly related to confidence in problem-solving (r = $-.39$) and to passivity (r = .28) (Table 4). No other coping strategies were significantly related to burden for either group of caregivers.

For both groups of caregivers, when the effect of age was controlled using analysis of covariance, caregivers who reported their own current health status to be poor had significantly higher passivity scores than caregivers who reported their health status to be fair to excellent (institutionalized $F(3,87) = 6.65$, community dwelling $F(3,135) = 8.01$). In both groups, use of the other seven coping strategies did not vary significantly by caregivers' health status levels.

DISCUSSION

The level of burden reported by caregivers in this study is similar to that reported in earlier studies (Zarit et al., 1981; Zarit, 1982). Caregiver burden scores were not significantly

Table 4

Correlation coefficients between Total Caregiver Burden and Coping
Strategies, Length of Caregiving, Caregiver Morale and Caregiver Age

	Patient Residence		
	Institution n=91	Community n=149	Total Sample n=240
Coping Strategies: Internal			
· Confidence in Problem-Solving	-.39*	-.06	-.19*
· Reframing	-.16	-.09	-.15*
· Passivity	.28*	.28*	.26*
Coping Strategies: External			
· Spiritual Support	-.17	-.26*	-.23*
· Extended Family	-.15	-.18*	-.16*
· Friends	.10	.09	.09
· Neighbors	-.16	.03	-.05
· Community Services	.16	.06	.11
Length of Caregiving	-.08	-.04	-.05
Caregiver Morale	-.49*	-.51*	-.49*
Caregiver Age	-.11	.01	-.04

*p≤.05

different between caregivers to community-dwelling or institutionalized patients. This indicates that the common belief that institutionalization abates the stress of caregiving may not be well-founded. However, some sources of burden were related to patient residence. Compared to caregivers to institutionalized patients, community caregivers gave significantly higher ratings to lack of privacy and time for self, negative impact on social relationships and the sense that their relative was dependent upon them. The sources of burden no doubt reflect the actual invasiveness of the caregiving role upon all other aspects of the caregiver's life. One caregiver eloquently expressed this experience:

> I was not prepared for the totality of the takeover; the presence of a dementia person (Alzheimer's disease) in the home and careprovider's life permeates everything, without exception. The careprovider no longer has a life of her/his own; the careprovider no longer has an identity of her/his own; insofar as our self-hood is defined by what we do, the careprovider has no opportunity to be anything but a careprovider. The careprovider must forego any hopes for her/his own future, since a hope is based upon the institutionalization or death of the Alzheimer's person . . . and this is inviting a massive guilt trip. (daughter, age 59)

Beyond expressing the strain of caregiving in the home, this caregiver also recognized the guilt that institutionalization of the patient may bring. Another caregiver, facing the decision about institutionalization, said:

> It is hard to know if what I am denied is justified. Would he be just as happy in a nursing home or is my sacrifice worthwhile? If it is worthwhile, I'll go on as long as possible but if it isn't, I'm not unaware that my life is draining away. (wife, age 58)

Caregivers to institutionalized patients reflected both guilt and ambivalence about institutional care. Compared to caregivers to community-dwelling patients, caregivers to institutionalized patients reported more frequently wishing they could leave caregiving to someone else and also more frequently sensing that they should be doing more. The poor physical health status of these caregivers very likely contributed to the decision to institutionalize the patient, a conclusion which is consistent with earlier studies (Tobin and Kulys, 1981; Brody, 1977). Similarly these caregivers perceived the patient to have more severe cognitive impairment than did caregivers to community-dwelling patients. Thus both the caregiver's health status and the patient's level of impairment would indicate that the decision for institutional care may have been based upon realistic assessments. Nevertheless, Brody (1977) has pointed out that "regardless of the most reality-based determinants of that placement," many caregivers experience tremendous guilt and perceive placement as a personal failure coming after months or years of caregiving with the aim of avoiding institutionalization. Some caregivers in this study captured these feelings in their statements about caregiving:

> Now that my husband is in the nursing home, I am lonely, but I just couldn't take care of him at home anymore—my back hurt constantly, I was cross with him and cried alot. (wife, age 71)

> The guilt feeling is still there even while recognizing the physical impossibility of continuing the care responsibility. After all, *she* nurtured we kids through total dependency, illness, and injury—why can't we do the same for her? (daughter, age 52)

> After providing care as long as possible and placing the victim in a nursing home and expecting to get some peace of mind, one sees all their assets being used up and a very bleak future, one envies the victim who is not conscious of their situation. (wife, age 76)

> There are no words to express the trauma of finally having to accept the fact that you cannot continue to care for him. (wife, age 74)

These quotes add further dimension to the empirical finding that burden was negatively correlated with morale and was significantly higher for caregivers who rated their health status as poor, regardless of the caregiver's age or patient's residence. These findings reinforce earlier studies in which caregivers to the disabled have been conceptualized as "hidden victims" (Fengler and Goodrich, 1979). Overall, 82 percent of the caregivers stated that caregiving had some negative effect on their own health status; almost half of caregivers to institutionalized patients and one third of the caregivers to community dwelling patients stated that this negative effect on their own health had been great. While caregiver age and pre-caregiving health status did not vary by patient residence, caregivers to institutionalized patients were significantly more likely to report lower levels of current health. This may indicate that these caregivers were particularly vulnerable to the health consequences of stress from caregiving.

Unfortunately no coping strategies investigated in this study were found to buffer the negative impact of caregiving upon physical health status. That is, use of positive psychological strategies (e.g., confidence, reframing) and social support was not related to caregiver's level of current health. On the other hand, passivity, characterized as an "avoidance response" (Olson et al., 1983) was used significantly more often by caregivers in poor or fair health, regardless of the caregiver's age. This finding may indicate that health status, not age, is the critical variable in the use of passivity as a coping strategy. Because of the cross-sectional design of this study, no causal statement can be made linking passivity to lower health status. It is probable that as health status declines, passivity increases. Future studies should further investigate the relationship of coping strategies to caregiver's health status, particularly because health status is clearly related to the caregivers' ability to provide continuing care in the community.

Because caregiver burden was related to several coping strategies, interventions may profitably improve or build upon strategies. Educational and other intervention programs should be designed to increase caregiver's confidence in problem-solving and provide caregivers help in redefining difficult situations. Caregivers to institutionalized patients who have low levels of confidence in problem-solving, appear to be particularly vulnerable to high levels of burden. Further, passivity which was positively related to burden, may be reduced if caregivers feel increased skills in caregiving and problem-solving.

Support from the extended family was associated with lower levels of burden for community caregivers. Professionals cannot assume that most caregivers can effectively identify and utilize family support resources. In fact, caregivers often have difficulty identifying what needs they have that others can meet as well as difficulty in identifying and utilizing other family members as sources of support (Springer and Brubaker, 1984). Education, support groups, and service programs should provide caregivers with encouragement and skills for effectively utilizing family support and should reach beyond the primary caregiver to educate other family members about the needs of both caregivers and patients.

Because spiritual support was helpful for many caregivers educating the religious community can be an important part of building support for caregivers. For some caregivers, spiritual support may provide meaning to the tremendous losses that accompany dementia. For example, one respondent commented that "this illness in the family is teaching me about my strengths and about how to gain strength from the Lord." Nevertheless, other caregivers expressed anger with God, questioning how such a devastating disease could affect their loved one. The caregiving experience may lead to what Mace and Robbins (1981) called a "spiritual crisis," that deprives caregivers of the strength that they previously received through faith. Clergy should be aware of the potential for both spiritual crisis and strength experienced by caregivers.

In summary, the potential psychological and physical impact of long-term care on caregivers must be recognized by health and social service agencies and policy makers. Given the high levels of burden, poor health and low morale found among relatives of institutionalized patients, it should not be assumed that family caregivers rebound from the strains of caregiving once the daily responsibilities are removed by institutionalization of the patient. Optimally, the institutions will serve the "family as a client" (Montgomery, 1983) and meet the family's needs as well as the patient's. Similarly, the needs of both patients and family caregivers should be addressed in designing community-based support groups and other interventions.

Future research should further examine the roles and interrelationships of psychological coping strategies and social support in protecting caregivers from the potentially negative psychological and physical consequences of caregiver. The current study reveals some fruitful directions for such research and clearly indicates the value of looking beyond demographic and caregiving characteristics in our attempts to understand caregiver burden.

BIBLIOGRAPHY

Archbold, P. G. (1982). All-consuming activity: the family as caregiver. *Generations, 7,* 12–13, 40.

Brody, E. M. (1977). *Long-term care of older people.* New York: Human Sciences Press.

Brody, E. M. & Lang, A. (1982). They can't do it all: Aging daughters with aged mothers. *Generations, 7,* 18–20, 37.

Carrilio, T. & Eisenberg, D. (1983). Informal resources for the elderly: panacea or empty promises. *Journal of Gerontological Social Work, 6* (1), 39–48.

Fengler, A. & Goodrich, N. (1979). Wives of elderly disabled men: the hidden patients. *The Gerontologist, 19* (2), 175–183.

Gwyther, L. P. & Matteson, M. A. (1983). Care for the caregivers. *Journal of Gerontological Nursing, 9,* 93–95, 110.

Lawton, M. P. (1971). The functional assessment of elderly people. *Journal of the American Geriatrics Society, 19* (6), 465–481.

Mace, N. & Robbins, P. (1981). *The 36-hour day.* Baltimore, MD: Johns Hopkins University Press.

McCubbin, H., Olson, D., & Larsen, A. (1981). Family crisis oriented personal evaluation scales (F-COPES). St. Paul, MN: Family Social Science, University of Minnesota.

Montgomery, R. (1983). Staff-family relations and institutional care policies. *Journal of Gerontological Social Work, 6* (1) 25–38.

Olson, D. H., McCubbin, H. I., Barnes, H., Larsen, A., Muxen, M., & Wilkson, M. (1983). *Families: What makes them work.* Beverly Hills, CA: Sage Publications.

Smith, K. F. & Bengston, V. L. (1979). Positive consequences of institutionalization: Solidarity between elderly partners and their middle-aged children. *Gerontologist, 19,* 438–447.

Springer, D. & Brubaker, T. (1984). *Family caregivers and dependent elderly: Minimizing stress and maximizing independence.* Beverly Hills, CA: Sage Publications.

Tobin, S. & Kulys, R. (1981). The family in the institutionalization of the elderly. *Journal of Social Issues, 37,* 145–157.

Zarit, J. M. (1982). Family role, social supports and their relation to caregivers' burden. Paper presented at the meeting of the Western Psychological Association, Sacramento, CA.

Zarit, J. M., Gatz, M., & Zarit, S. H. (1981). Family relationships and burden in long-term care. Paper presented at the meetings of the Gerontological Society, Toronto, Ontario.

Zarit, S. H., Reever, K. E., & Bach-Peterson, J. (1980). Relatives of the impaired elderly: Correlates of feelings of burden. *Gerontologist, 20,* 649–655.

Zarit, S. H. & Zarit, J. M. (1982). Families under stress: Interventions for caregivers of senile dementia patients. *Psychotherapy: Theory, Research and Practice, 19,* 461–471.

Factors Associated With the Configuration of the Helping Networks of Noninstitutionalized Elders

Raymond T. Coward, PhD

ABSTRACT. Telephone interviews were conducted with a sample of noninstitutionalized elders (n = 900) regarding the help they received with four tasks: transportation; home repair and maintenance; household chores; and personal health care. Respondents indicated that the vast majority (70.0%) of the nonspousal helpers from whom aid was being received were from the informal network and affirmed the prevalence of family members as helpers (83.2% of the informal helpers named were family). The age, gender, marital status, health and life satisfaction of the elders were all found to be significantly associated with differences in the configurations of the helping networks that surrounded the respondents. The implications of the data for social work research and practice are discussed.

Dr. Coward is Professor of Social Work, The University of Vermont, Burlington, VT 05405–0160. This manuscript was developed under the auspices of Regional Research Project NE-131 funded by the U.S. Department of Agriculture, the Northeast Regional Center for Rural Development, and the Agricultural Experiment Stations of New Hampshire, New Jersey, Maine, Pennsylvania, Vermont and West Virginia. The opinions expressed in this document, however, do not necessarily reflect the positions of those organizations and no official endorsement should be inferred. As chairperson of the Technical Committee advising the project, the author gratefully acknowledges the contributions of those who have served from the beginning to guide the focus of the research and to provide leadership to all aspects of the data collection: Robert A. Bylund, Charles O. Crawford, Donn A. Derr, Robert W. Jackson, Edmund F. Jensen, Jr., Kenneth D. McIntosh, Rex H. Warland and Dennis A. Watkins. In addition, Lotte Marcus, Eloise Rathbone-McCuan and Gary R. Lee critiqued earlier versions of this manuscript and their contributions and recommendations were sincerely appreciated. Finally, the author acknowledges the useful input of the anonymous reviewers. Parts of this article were presented at an invited lecture before the Committee for Studies on Aging of McGill University (Montreal, PQ, Canada).

Over the past decade gerontological social workers have become increasingly aware of the magnitude and pervasiveness of help received by elders from their social support networks (Cohen and Rajkowski, 1982; Kohen, 1983; Moon, 1983). Despite the reality of isolation for a small, but nevertheless disturbing number of elders (Rathbone-McCuan and Hashimi, 1982), current research has demonstrated that the vast majority of the elderly are embedded in a social support network that provides significant help and assistance with the tasks of daily living (Bair and Hiltner, 1982; Powers and Bultena, 1974; Shanas, 1979; Stoller and Earl, 1983).

Within the social support networks of older people, the family is an essential and dominant element—providing a wide range of help under a variety of circumstances. The empirical support for the significant role of the family as helpers to the elderly is in contrast to the popular myths of family abandonment and family alienation, but is now firmly established by the repeated observations of many scholars (Kohen, 1983; Stoller and Earl, 1983; Weeks and Cuellar, 1981). For elders with marital partners, most often the spouse is the major source of aid. Moreover, this spousal caregiving does not seem to be constrained by gender; when necessary, older men with disabled wives will assume what for many are the unfamiliar chores of housework (Hess and Soldo, in press). Crossman, Landon and Barry (1981) have reported data indicating that the spouse is the most likely primary caregiver for those impaired elders who live in the community and require long-term care. Indeed, "the frail elderly cared for at home by spouses are generally more impaired than those cared for by other relatives and friends" (Hess and Soldo, in press, p. 18).

When the spouse is not available, or their ability to provide help is severely limited, other family members—primarily adult children—are the principal sources of help. Stoller (1983) noted that adult children were nearly half (47%) of the first helpers named by her linear probability sample of noninstitutionalized elders in upstate New York (n = 753). There seems to be evidence for a strong sense of filial responsibility among many American families and adult children frequently provide valuable social-emotional support, monetary and financial aid, and/or assistance with the tasks of daily living.

Research has also established that friends and neighbors can be an important component of the mixture of informal help that surrounds elders (Bair and Hiltner, 1982; Stoller and Earl, 1983); although the amount of such assistance is generally considerably smaller and of a different kind than that provided by family members. For those who lack a wide network of family ties (e.g., the never-married, the childless, or the frail widow) or whose family relationships are strained (due to geographical distance or a history of negative interactions); neighbors and friends may represent a major component of the helping network (Hooyman, 1983).

The prominence and significance of the informal network as helpers to the elderly, however, does not dimish the crucial role of the services provided by formal helpers and those agencies that offer aid to the elderly. For those elders who are not immersed in a social network which provides support and assistance, the availability of formal services is especially critical to maintaining their quality of life. For those elders who do have an informal helping network at their disposal, formal services are more often a decisive complement to the informal network which permits the elders to maximize their independence and the quality of their lives (Eustis, Greenberg and Patten, 1984). In a sample of elders from New York City who applied for homemaker services, for example, 82% reported that they believed their families were doing all they could for them; yet, 62% acknowledged that the services they received from formal helpers permitted them "to continue to live independently in the community" (Lewis, Bienenstock, Cantor and Schneewind, 1980, p. 8).

Recent reports from both researchers and practitioners have indicated that some elders meet their needs for support and aid by combining the resources available through both the informal and formal networks. Data from the Home Care Supplement to the 1979 National Health Interview Survey, for example, found that 15.9% of a large, national sample of elders with functional limitations reported receiving aid from a mixture of formal and informal care providers (Center for Population Research, 1980). Similarly, from a smaller area sample of a more general population of elders, Stoller and Earl (1983) noted that approximately 6% of their respondents reported receiving aid from a mixed network of formal and informal helpers. The difference in the proportion of the elders who reported the use of mixed configurations is probably a function of the sampling techniques used in the two projects—Stoller and Earl (1983) used a probability sample (thus including a wider variation of life circumstances and needs) whereas the Center for Population Research (1980) study concentrated on elders with functional limitations.

As the life circumstances, health, physical abilities and mobility of elders change, it has been suggested that the relative role of children, kin, friends and formal helpers will vary. Indeed, Kahn (1979) has proposed the term "social convoy" to reflect the dynamic aspect of social support relationships. Yet, there are significant voids in even our most elementary understanding of the characteristics or circumstances of the elderly which are associated with different forms or configurations of the helping network. In addition, our knowledge base needs to be expanded beyond a concentration on the dependent, frail elderly who have severe impairments and begin to encompass an appreciation of the dynamics of helping relationships in the more general, noninstitutionalized population of aged in the United States.

Specifically, more clarity is needed on the following basic elements: (1) What is the relative prevalence of different combinations of informal and formal helping in the social support networks of noninstitutionalized elders? and (2) What characteristics of the elderly are associated with the different configurations of the helping networks that can be observed? Data on these elementary, descriptive indicators of the interplay between formal and informal networks will enlarge the empirical base from which service providers can create interventions which maximize the strengths of each resource. The research project described in the following sections was directed at illuminating more fully the relative role of formal and informal helpers in the lives of a random sample of elders living in the community.

METHODS

Sampling Procedures

Eighteen sites were selected for study, from a universe of all of the minor civil divisions (n = 3,338) in six Northeastern states. Communities were randomly chosen for study using a sampling framework stratified on three variables: (1) residence: metropolitan or nonmetropolitan according to the 1980 Census; (2) community size: using the 1980 size of population, communities were classified into three categories (less than 2,500 persons; 2,500 to 19,999 persons, and more than 20,000 persons); and (3) community growth pattern: comparing population size in 1970 to that in 1980, communities were classified as either declining (those that experienced a loss in population that was 10% or more) stable (those that had a change in population that was less than 10% loss or gain) and expanding (those that had a gain in population of 10% or more).

Because of the geographical dispersion of the sample, the difficulty of residence-based random selection procedures in nonmetropolitan environments, and the high cost of personal interviews, data were collected via the telephone. A form of random digit dialing was used in each community to place telephone calls or, where appropriate, an alternative procedure more congruent with the locale was identified for the random telephoning of households. Calls were made until completed interviews were conducted with 50 individuals over the age of 65 years who resided in each of the communities of interest. The procedures resulted in a total sample size of 900 persons. (50 persons/community × 18 different communities).

Interviewing Procedures

Field work on the study began in September 1982 and was concluded in five months. A structured interviewing protocol was used which included both open-ended and fixed-response questions. The average length of an interview was 24.6 minutes (interviews ranged from 12 to 70 minutes). The protocol focused on help provided to the elderly in four task areas considered critical to the daily quality of life of elders: (1) personal health care including the taking of medicine and other activities related to non-acute illnesses; (2) transportation to needed destinations; (3) routine home repair and maintenance work like putting up storm windows, touch-up painting or replacing a worn electrical switch; and (4) indoor household chores such as cooking, cleaning and laundry. In each of the four task areas, elders were asked to identify all individuals from whom they were receiving help. Detailed information (including sex, age, relationship to helper and details of the help that was being provided) was collected on the first two helpers that were named by the elder in each task area.[1]

A total of 6,858 telephone numbers were randomly selected and dialed to identify individuals eligible for the study. Eligibility required the individual to meet certain criteria: (1) the household had to be located in one of the 18 communities selected for study; (2) the individual selected had to reside most of the year in the household contacted (i.e., not just visiting); (3) the individual had to be aged 65 years or older; and (4) in households where there was more than one elder, selection of which elder to interview was made by employing a predetermined procedure for random selection. Of the 1,308 elders determined eligible, 68.8% completed the interview protocol and 23.4% refused to participate. The other eligible elders were either unable to come to the phone (4.4%), started the interview but did not finish (2.6%), agreed to participate but could not be reached by call backs (0.5%), or were not going to be available during the period of time the study was to be completed (0.2%).

Sample

The average age of respondents was 72.64 years (range was 65 to 96 years). The sample was composed almost entirely of Whites (94.4%). There were more females than males in the sample—65.4% to 34.6%—and more widows and widowers (46.3%) than elders with living marital partners (44.0%). The majority of the respondents considered themselves to be in good health (60.1% rated their health status as good or very good). More than half of the sample (57.7%) had not completed the twelfth grade and very few (7.9%) had a college degree. Incomes ranged from less than $200 a month to more than $1,501 per month, with the median and modal income being $501 to $800 a month. Respondents reported a mean life satisfaction of 8.18 (standard deviation = 1.18) on a scale where 10.0 was the highest ranking. Table 1 contains the distribution of selected descriptive statistics on the sample.

Table 1: Distribution of Selected Personal Characteristics of the Elderly Respondents

Personal Characteristics	Number of Respondents	Percentage
Age		
65-74	552	61.6
75-84	289	32.3
85+	55	6.1
Sex		
Males	311	34.6
Females	589	65.4
Marital Status		
Never Married	45	5.0
Married	396	44.0
Widowed	417	46.3
Divorced/Separated	42	4.7
Education		
Less than 8th Grade	169	18.9
8th - 11th Grade	347	38.8
High School Graduate	205	22.9
Post Secondary	173	19.4
Monthly Income		
Up to $200	9	1.1
$201 - 300	29	3.5
$301 - 400	101	12.2
$401 - 500	223	26.9
$501 - 800	251	30.2
$801 - 1,000	122	14.7
$1,001 - 1,500	43	5.2
Greater than $1,501	52	6.3
Health Status		
Very Good	222	24.7
Good	318	35.4
Fair	242	26.9
Poor	69	7.7
Very Poor	48	5.3
Life Satisfaction		
1 - Very Dissatisfied	2	0.2
2-3-4	18	2.2
5-6	134	16.2
7-8-9	403	48.6
10 - Very Satisfied	272	32.8

RESULTS

Magnitude of the Helping Network

The 900 elders interviewed in this sample identified 1,939 individuals other than their spouse who were providing help in at least one of the task areas about which the survey inquired.[2] Of this total helping network, detailed records were collected on the first two helpers named by each elder (if that many were named) in each task area. As a result, on 1,301 helpers (or 67.1% of all the helpers named) comprehensive records existed that included their sex, age, relationship to the elder, and details about the assistance that they provided.

The analyses reported below focus on the subsample of the full helping network on which detailed information was collected. The dependent variable has been constructed by aggregating all the help received in the four task areas that were the focus of this study (i.e., personal health care, routine home repair and maintenance, transportation and indoor household chores) in order to examine the makeup and configurations of the helping network in its entirety. It should be noted, however, that other analyses of this data set have confirmed that significant differences exist in the magnitude and composition of nonspousal help as a function of the task being performed (Crawford, Goodfellow and Warland, 1984).

The vast majority (70.0%) of the nonspousal helpers on which detailed information was collected were from the informal helping network. Those elders that reported receiving help from the informal network (526 or 58.4% of the sample), named an average of 1.73 informal helpers from whom they were receiving aid (standard deviation = .85).

For those elders that reported receiving help from the formal network (290 or 32.2% of the sample), a mean of 1.34 formal helpers were identified (standard deviation = .66). This category was not comprised entirely of recipients of public aid. The formal helpers category in this study included both community agency personnel and private sector individuals who received a fee for their services (e.g., an electrician in the area of home repairs and maintenance or a private nurse in the area of personal health care).

About one-quarter of the sample (25.4% or 228 elders) reported receiving no help from anyone other than their spouse, if one was present, in the four task areas under investigation. For the most part this category did not seem to be comprised of elders with significant unmet needs. For example, when those that were performing the tasks alone were asked if this constituted a problem or a burden, the overwhelming majority indicated that it was not—the highest percentage of elders that indicated that doing tasks alone was a problem was in the area of household chores (7.2%) and the lowest percentage was in home repairs and maintenance (2.0%).

Compositions of the Helping Network

The various combinations of help that was being received can be categorized into four mutually exclusive patterns of helping network composition. The most prevalent pattern of caregiving that was identified was the receipt of help exclusively from informal helpers; 371 elders or 41.4% of the sample were in this category. Receiving help from only the informal network was almost twice as likely as the next most frequent pattern—which was to receive help from no non-spousal helpers (238 elders or 26.6% of the sample reported this pattern). The third most widespread pattern reported was the receipt of aid from a mixture, or combination, of formal and informal helpers, 154 elders or 17.2% of the sample were in this pattern. The least likely pattern to be identified, 14.8% of the total sample, was a network comprised of only formal helpers.

Associations Between Characteristics of the Elderly Respondents and Different Helping Network Configurations

Tables 2 and 3 present data comparing the distribution of selected characteristics of the elderly respondents across the four configurations of helping networks discussed above. Where data were nominal in nature, comparisons were made using the chi-square calculation (Table 2); in contrast, when data were ordinally scaled, comparisons were made using the analysis of variance technique (Table 3).

Age

Data in Table 3 indicate that as age increased there was a tendency towards the greater use of both formal and informal helpers. Respondents who reported receiving no help had the lowest average age (69.99 years) and the next youngest respondents were those using only formal helpers (72.54 years). Those elders reporting the receipt of help simultaneously from both formal and informal helpers had the highest average age of any of the patterns observed (75.58 years).

Table 2:   Chi-Square Comparisons of Selected Personal Characteristics of the Elderly
           Respondents By Helping Network Configuration.

Variable	Total Sample	No Help	Informal Helpers Only	Mixed Helpers	Formal Helpers Only	Chi Square
Sex						
Males	34.6 (311)*	41.2	36.7	9.3	12.9	59.85**
Females	65.4 (589)	18.7	43.8	21.2	16.3	
Marital Status						
Never Married	5.0 (45)	11.1	40.0	20.0	28.9	
Married	44.0 (396)	47.0	30.6	11.4	11.1	166.63**
Widowed	46.3 (417)	8.4	51.8	22.3	17.5	
Divorced/Separated	4.7 (42)	28.6	40.5	16.7	14.3	
Functional Health						
Great Difficulty	22.0 (197)	13.7	44.2	26.4	15.7	
Some	25.6 (230)	22.6	39.6	21.3	16.5	50.68**
Very Little	24.5 (220)	30.5	44.1	12.7	12.7	
Not At All	27.9 (250)	36.8	38.0	9.6	15.6	

*   The figures in parenthesis represent the number of respondents in each category. Total
    sample size for each variable will fluctuate as a function of the number of respondents
    who answered each item.

**   Probability < .001

Gender

Data in Table 2 indicate that there was less than a .001 probability that the observed distributions for gender would occur. The helping networks surrounding the female respondents were much more likely to include formal helpers—37.5% of the female respondents reported some use of formal helpers, whereas 22.2% of the males reported receiving formal help. Similarly, whereas nearly half of the males (41.2%) received no assistance from nonspousal helpers, only 18.7% of the females were in this situation.

Marital Status

Those with marital partners reported distinctly different helping patterns than any of the other categories of respondents. A much higher percentage of the married respondents (47.0%) reported receiving no nonspousal help with the tasks that were studied—for example, their rate of response in the

Table 3: Comparisons of Selected Personal Characteristics of the Elderly Respondents by Helping Network Configuration.

Variable	Total Sample	No Help	Informal Helpers Only	Mixed Helpers Only	Formal Helpers Only	F
Age of Elder	Mean 72.64 (896)* S.D. 6.20	69.99 (238) 4.81	73.15 (371) 6.45	75.58 (154) 6.24	72.54 (133) 5.81	29.48**
Life Satisfaction	Mean 8.18 (829) S.D. 1.81	8.40 (225) 1.61	8.06 (342) 1.91	7.96 (132) 1.87	8.35 (130) 1.76	2.64***
Perceived Stress from Health Problems	Mean .72 (894) S.D. 1.17	.55 (236) 1.08	.77 (370) 1.20	.98 (153) 1.30	.55 (135) 1.05	5.33**

* The figures in parenthesis represent the number of respondents in each category. Total sample size for each variable will fluctuate as a function of the number of respondents who answered each item.

** Probability <.001

*** Probability <.05

"no help" category was nearly six times greater than that of widowed elders in the sample. Additionally, the use of formal helpers by married respondents was much smaller than that of respondents in the other marital categories. Nearly half (48.9%) of the never married respondents, for instance, had formal helpers involved in their helping networks—a rate that was double that of the married elders.

Health

Analyses in Tables 2 and 3 include two indicators of the relationship between health and helping patterns. From Table 2, the data indicate that as perceived functional health is judged to be a greater barrier in performing the tasks of daily living, the number of elders reporting receipt of no help declines and the percentage using mixed networks of formal and informal helpers increases linearly. In Table 3, there is also a progression of greater perceived stress from health related problems as comparisons are made starting from respondents receiving no help (.55) or only help from formal providers (.55), to those using informal helpers only (.77), and finally to those using mixed networks of formal and informal helpers (.98).

Life Satisfaction

Respondents reporting the receipt of no aid from nonspousal helpers or the use of only formal helpers reported the highest average ratings of life satisfaction (8.40 and 8.35 respectively). In contrast, those that were using both formal and informal helpers to meet their needs in the four task areas studied, had the lowest average ratings (7.96). As is common in the life satisfaction scales of this type, the uniformly high ratings of American elders needs to be acknowledged (Tremblay, Walker and Dillman, 1983) and, therefore, differences between groups kept in perspective.

One final observation should be noted on all of the analyses which are contained in Tables 2 and 3. Although the univariate procedures employed have demonstrated the significant associations between age, gender, marital status, health and life satisfaction and the configurations of helping that were observed, it should be pointed out that there are also statistically significant relationships *between* some of these variables. For example, women in the sample tended to be older and were more apt to be widowed—all of which were factors that in this sample were associated with differences in the configurations of the helping networks in which they participated. Table 4 presents the correlations between the selected characteristics of the elderly that were examined in Tables 2 and 3. The magnitude of these correlations are modest (particularly given the large size of the sample); nevertheless, these inter-relationships should be considered as interpretations of the data are rendered and future research will need to accommodate these covariations.

DISCUSSION

This exploration into the relative role of formal and informal helpers in the lives of a sample of noninstitutionalized elders has provided some further illumination of the structural dynamics surrounding caregiving in later life. In certain respects, these data have provided further empirical support for

Table 4: Pearson Product-Movement Correlations Between Selected Personal Characteristics of the Elderly Respondents.

	Age	Gender	Marital Status	Functional Health
Gender	.17*	--	--	--
Marital Status	.19*	.28*	--	--
Functional Health	-.09**	-.02	-.05	--
Life Satisfaction	.09**	.01	-.10**	.18*

* > .001

** > .05

well established characterizations of the life circumstances of American elders (e.g., the significant role of informal helpers as caregivers to the elderly). Conversely, the data also offer new insights into the complex web of social networks that aid the elderly (e.g., the prominence of mixed networks of formal and informal helpers in the lives of the elders in the sample). In the sections below, some of the implications of these data for social work research and practice are examined.

Independent Elders

The data from this survey serve to remind us of the significant number of elders—25.4% in this sample—who are able to meet entirely their needs without the help of anyone beyond themselves and their marital partner if one exists (78.2% of the elders who reported receiving no help with the four task areas that were investigated had marital partners living with them). Data from Tables 2 and 3 indicate that those elders who were not receiving help tended to be younger, male, living with a marital partner, healthier and reported higher levels of life satisfaction.

This population of able elders represents an important resource for their communities, their families and for themselves. Hooyman (1983) has illustrated that able elders are becoming an increasingly utilized resource in the delivery of services to other elders. Elders are now used in service agencies across the country as peer counselors, outreach workers, visiting companions, ombudsmen and social advocates. In addition, there has been a surge in the number of mutual help groups among the elderly (e.g., Widow-to-Widow programs, stroke clubs and Alzheimer support groups), emphasizing joint problem solving, mutual care, and elders helping elders. Hooyman (1983) has collected a number of examples of attempts by formal agencies to enhance and facilitate the exchange of help between elders and to use able elders as caregivers to the more dependent aged.

Most gerontological social workers are well aware that this cohort of able elders exists and that to some extent a portion of them are prepared to provide aid to others; however, it is less clear how a service provider or agency goes about harnessing that energy. There is a critical need, therefore, for gerontological social work to refine and articulate precisely the processes, techniques and practice skills that are required to create, organize and sustain an artificially constructed network of elders helping other elders or to support such caregiving where it exits naturally.

Moreover, future research must define the full implications for the elder of become a helper to another elder. That is, there are some positive benefits that will certainly accrue to the helper as a function of their participation in such relationships (e.g., enhanced self concept from contributing to the needs of others; or, the ability to maintain a sense of worthiness from continuing to participate and contribute to meaningful activities); nevertheless, we also know that informal helping relationships have a darker side (Coward, 1982)—one that includes feelings of burdens under which artifically created networks of elders helping elders are most effective and to demarcate the realistic limits of such relationships.

Informal Help

The findings of this investigation into the helping networks that surround elders living independently in the community are consistent with the ever-growing segment of literature that affirms the prominence and significance of the natural support system. Moreover, this investigation also corroborates the continued preeminent role of the family as the major force in the informal helping network and as the principle component of the total helping network. More than eighty percent (83.2%) of the informal helpers that were named were family members—this represented 759 of the 1,301 helpers for whom there was data on their relationship to the elder or 58.3% of the total helping network. Indeed, adult children alone comprised nearly half (47.6%) of the informal helping network and one-third (33.4%) of the total helping system. Once again there is empirical evidence for the assertion that many American families have not abandoned their elders or abdicated their responsibilities to their loved ones.

Although the data from this survey are of a cross-sectional nature, they imply that there may be a threshold to the amount of caregiving that can be provided by the informal network acting alone. For example, as functional health became a greater barrier to performing the tasks of daily living (see Table 2), the percentage of elders reporting the receipt of help from only the informal network remained relatively stable (the range was from a low of 38.0% to a high of 44.2%). In contrast (although as would be expected), as health became a greater functional barrier, the major shifts seemed to occur in the dramatic decrease in the number of elders receiving no aid from nonspousal helpers (from a high of 36.8% to a low of 13.7%) and the substantial increase in the proportion reporting the use of mixed networks of both formal and informal helpers (for a low of 9.6% to a high of 26.4%).

Whether or not there is a threshold beyond which the informal helping network is unable (or unwilling) to fulfill the needs of their elderly loved ones entirely by themselves will only be determined by conducting longitudinal studies which follow the progression of caregiving throughout the lives of a cohort of elders. Similarly, the data from this investigation are unable to determine the stability of the composition of the informal helping network under changing conditions faced by the elderly (e.g., increasing age, declines in functional health status or sudden acute health crises). That is, these cross sectional data reflect a degree of stability in the relative prevalence or magnitude of the informal helping network acting alone across different circumstances; however, because this was not a longitudinal sample these data are unable to address the question of the stability of the composition of the informal network. Do the same individuals remain part of the "social convoy" or, over time and under changing circumstances, are they replaced by other members of the informal network? Is there "burnout" for informal helpers? To determine the exact progression and direction of these potential shifting patterns of responsibility will also require the implementation and completion of longitudinal studies.

Mixed Networks

The data from these interviews confirm that as increases occur in those variables generally associated with higher levels of disability (e.g., widowhood and functional health in Table 2 or age and perceived health stress in Table 3), there is an increase in the number of formal helpers involved in the network. The data also demonstrated that a significant number of the total sample of respondents (17.2%) were utilizing simultaneously the services of both formal and informal helpers. This percentage is higher than reported in previous research (Center for Population Research, 1980; Stoller and Earl, 1983) and most probably is the result, in part, of differences in the classification of formal and informal helpers.[3]

Respondents that were simultaneously using formal and informal helpers were disproportionately older, female, widowed, experiencing greater amounts of stress and difficulties performing the tasks of daily living as a function of their health problems and reporting lower levels of life satisfaction. Given this profile of personal characteristics, combined with our current understanding of the demographics of aging in the United States (e.g., that elders over the age of 80 years are the fastest growing segment of the aged population and that this age group experiences the greatest prevalence of physical disability), we can speculate that the use of mixed networks of helpers is likely to increase in the near future. As a consequence, the dynamics of the relationship between these two sources of help, only narrowly examined in this data set, will need to be illuminated more fully before service providers have a sufficient base from which to inform practice.

Furthermore, the total number of helpers who are providing aid to the elderly is an additional dimension of the helping network that needs to be considered. Although the vast majority (80.9%) of the elders in this sample had three or less helpers providing assistance (combining both formal and informal networks), the remainder of the sample had up to fourteen different helpers involved. For this smaller segment of the sample who use a wide array of helpers (about one in every five elders), there were a substantial number of interpersonal relationships and schedules to be coordinated and manipulated. Moreover, in those networks that are a combination of formal and informal helpers, the complexity of this coordination may be exacerbated by the divergent goals and perspectives of the two systems.

Further research is needed to illuminate the impact on the quality of life and day-to-day functioning of elders who participate in these large and diverse helping networks. In addition, research is needed to examine more fully the influence of the type of help that is needed by the elder on the configuration of the helping network that responds to that need.

SUMMARY

This descriptive study of the helping networks surrounding elders has served to illustrate, once again, the complexity that exists in these relationships. If gerontological social workers are going to be able to develop complementary functions and activities between formal and informal helping networks which serve to enhance further the quality of life of elders, research efforts to illuminate the factors that explain the interpersonal dynamics that underlie these relationships must be continued. This is not to suggest that social workers should cease their attempts to create collaborative relationships between formal and informal helpers; however, endeavors must be undertaken cautiously until a better understanding of the relative role of the two systems is developed.

REFERENCE NOTES

1. The interviewing protocol asked respondents first to name "who does most" in the particular task area that was being discussed. After detailed information was collected on the first helper named, the interviewer asked "does anyone else help" with the particular task area that was being discussed. If a second helper was named, detailed information was also collected on that person. If there were more than two helpers from whom aid was being received in a particular task area, the interviewer asked "how many other people help" with the task area being discussed. Using these procedures, detailed information were collected on 1,301 individuals or 67.1% of all the helpers named.

2. Recent research has made it clear that the helping networks and help seeking behaviors of married elders are quite different from those patterns that form around elders who are without partners (Hess and Soldo, in press; Stoller and Earl, 1983). Indeed, the analysis reported in Table 2 reflects this pattern for the sample studied in this research. When marital partners are available and able they often act as the primary source of help. Although 44.0% of this sample were married, more than three-quarters (78.2%) of those reporting the use of no nonspousal helpers were married. Nevertheless, we must also be aware that many elders do not have such sources of help available to them. As a consequence, it is critical for researchers to examine the extended nonspousal helping network and to illuminate its character and

nature. Therefore, the focus of the analysis here will be on the informal and formal help received beyond the marital bond.

3. As research on caregiving networks increases and matures, the need for a standardized system to classify formal and informal helpers is intensified. Currently, the literature contains a wide range of classification systems and, therefore, comparisons between different samples and projects are made more difficult or, in some instances, impossible.

REFERENCES

Blair, C. W. and Hiltner, J. *The Independent Elderly: Medical and Social Service Needs and Use by Older Persons in Northwest Ohio.* Toledo, Ohio: Department of Medicine, Medical College of Ohio, 1982.

Center for Population Research. *Tabulations from the 1979 Health Interview Survey, Home Care Supplement.* Prepared under subcontract to the Urban Institute for the Department of Health and Human Services, Office of the Assistant Secretary for Planning and Evaluation, Contract No. HHS-100-80-0158, 1980.

Cohen, C. I. and Rajkowski, H. What's in a friend? Substantive and theoretical issues. *The Gerontologist,* 1982, 22(3), 261–266.

Coward, R. T. "Cautions about the role of natural helping networks in programs for the rural elderly." In N. Stinnett, J. DeFrain, K. King, H. Lingren, G. Rowe, S. Van Zandt and R. Williams (Eds.). *Family Strengths 4: Positive Support Systems.* Lincoln: The University of Nebraska Press, 1982, 291–306.

Crawford, C. O., Goodfellow, M. and Warland, R. H. Characteristics of help users and of helpers. Paper presented at the 4th Annual Conference of the Northeastern Gerontological Society, Philadelphia, April 1984.

Crossman, L., Landon, C. and Barry, C. Older women caring for disabled spouses: A model for supportive services. *The Gerontologist,* 1981, 21, 464–470.

Eustis, N. N., Greenberg, J. N. and Patten, S. K. *Long-Term Care for Older Persons: A Policy Perspective.* Monterey, California: Brooks/Cole Publishing Company, 1984.

Hess, B. B. and Soldo, B. J. "Husband and wife networks." In W. J. Sauer and R. T. Coward (Eds.), *Social Support Networks and the Care of the Elderly: Theory, Research and Practice.* New York: Springer Publishing Company, in press.

Hooyman, N. "Social support networks in services to the elderly." In Whittaker, J. K. and Garbarino, J. (Eds.), *Social Support Networks: Informal Helping in the Human Services.* New York: Aldine Publishing Company, 1983, p. 133–164.

Kahn, R. L. "Aging and social support." In M. W. Riley (Ed.), *Aging from Birth to Death.* Boulder, Colorado: Westview Press, 1979.

Kohen, J. A. Old but not alone: Informal social supports among the elderly by marital status and sex. *The Gerontologist,* 1983, 23(1), 56–63.

Lewis, M., Bienenstock, R., Cantor, M. and Schneewind, E. The extent to which informal and formal supports interact to maintain older people in the community. Paper presented at the Annual Meetings of the Gerontological Society of America, San Diego, California, 1980.

Moon, M. The role of the family in the economic well-being of the elderly. *The Gerontologist.* 1983, 23(1), 45–50.

Powers, E. and Bultena, G. Correspondence between anticipated and actual uses of public services by the aged. *Social Services Review.* 1974, 48, 245–254.

Rathbone-McCuan, E. and Hashimi, J. *Isolated Elders: Health and Social Intervention.* Rockville, Maryland: Aspen Systems Corporation, 1982.

Shanas, E. The family as a social support system in old age. *The Gerontologist,* 1979, 19, 169–174.

Stoller, E. P. Parental caregiving by adult children. *Journal of Marriage and the Family,* 1983, 45(4), 851–858.

Stoller, E. P. and Earl, L. L. Help with activities of everyday life: Source of support for the noninstitutionalized elderly. *The Gerontologist,* 1983, 23(1), 64–70.

Weeks, J. R. and Cuellar, J. B. The role of family members in the helping networks of older people. *The Gerontologist,* 1981, 21(4), 388–394.

Racial Differences in Family Burden: Clinical Implications for Social Work

Richard K. Morycz, PhD, ACSW
Julie Malloy, ACSW
Maryann Bozich, MSW
Pamela Martz, BA

ABSTRACT. This article examines the clinical implications for social work practice of the differential impact of caregiving strain according to race. Data for this report is drawn from a study of 810 patients in a community-based geriatric assessment center. Although this research found no essential difference, based on race, in the experience of family burden as a social problem, there was a difference within the interaction of race and the care for an elderly person with Alzheimer's disease. The authors suggest a classification schema of specific interventions for different caregiving groups and subgroups, based on both race and relationship; these selected variables can provide more insight into possible vulnerable caregiving conditions.

I. INTRODUCTION AND REVIEW OF PROBLEM

Increasingly sophisticated efforts for studying the burden on families caring for older members with Alzheimer's disease have provided social workers with potentially useful tools and clues for assessment and intervention. Several research proj-

This research was partially supported by a grant from the Claude Worthington Benedum Foundation; it was presented at the 37th Annual Meeting of the Gerontological Society of America, San Antonio, Texas, November, 1984. Reprint requests should be addressed to Richard K. Morycz, PhD, ACSW, Assistant Professor of Psychiatry & Medicine, University of Pittsburgh School of Medicine and Program Director, Benedum Geriatric Center, 3601 Fifth Avenue, Pittsburgh, PA 15213.

133

ects have focused on the differential impact of caregiving strain according to age (Gonyea and Montgomery, 1984), gender (Todd et al., 1984; Fitting, 1984), relationship (Deimling, 1984), or race (Morycz et al., 1984) of the patient or caregiver. Family burden assessment instruments have been developed, pilot-tested, and utilized in both research and clinical settings (see, for example, Zarit, 1982; Morycz, 1982 and 1985; Niederche et al., 1982; Wilder et al., 1983). These studies have overcome some of the deficits of earlier research and now include larger sample sizes, multivariate analyses and a more consistent and concise use of terminology (for example, see Deimling).

There has been little work, however on studying caregivers with diverse racial and ethnic backgrounds to determine if there are racial differences, and to assess whether those differences are (as Jackson, in 1967, noted) differences of degree rather than of kind. Although Henderson (1984) has tried to focus attention on developing culturally-relevant intervention strategies for elderly people of racial and ethnic minorities coping with Alzheimer's disease, there has been a dearth of data exploring differential approaches. The Department of Health and Human Services Task Force on Alzheimer's disease has urged increased study about how and in what ways different family members are affected by a relative with Alzheimer's disease, and whether certain effects and stress factors can be predicted based on caregiver characteristics (see Ory et al., 1984).

Summary of Research. A variety of research reports have emphasized a powerful kinship network in black families (Jackson, 1980; Gelfand, 1982). Also, black families have been found to rely on extended kin to a greater extent than white families in times of crisis (cf. Wylie, 1971; Martin and Martin, 1978; Haveven, 1980; and Devore, 1983), Cantor (1979a and b) and Bengston (1978) have noted that black aged have increasing help from adult offspring, especially daughters (e.g., see Jackson, 1971).

Families are the primary source of care for white and black elderly (Shanas, 1979; Sheldon, 1982; Schultz and Rau, 1985); the purpose of this paper is to examine the clinical implications for social work practice with white and black caregiving groups of the functionally disabled elderly, and more specifically, of Alzheimer's disease patients. This discussion of clinical practice interventions is based on a study of over 800 patients in a community-based geriatric assessment center in Pittsburgh. Specific findings of this research were first presented at the 37th Annual Meeting of the Gerontological Society of America, San Antonio, Texas (1984). A brief summary of methods and results is presented here.

Comprehensive chart review of 815 patients included information on patient demographics, clinical characteristics, social support systems, and data bases from multidisciplinary evaluations; such data bases included a complete medical history and physical assessment, laboratory screening tests, a structured psychosocial interview, a Folstein Mini-Mental State examination (Folstein et al., 1975), the OARS Multidimensional Functional Assessment (Pfeiffer, 1975—that includes questions on both instrumental and physical activities of daily living), and a family burden instrument (Morycz, 1982, 1985). This burden instrument contains a caretaking difficulty index that assesses change in caregiver feeling states, living patterns, and relationships.

In this research, family burden was found to be a social problem in about one-quarter of all cases (Morycz et al., 1984). Table 1 summarizes sample characteristics of the 815 patients in this study, by race. Black elderly patients comprise nearly 12% of the total patient population, and this is representative of this geographic area. The average patient was a 75-year-old, widowed woman; this was true for both black and white groups. In fact, characteristics of black and white groups are quite similar. For instance, slightly over 30% of black and white patients live alone. Also, about 20% of patients are cared for by spouses, and 20% by daughters. The score on the Folstein Mini-Mental State Examination was 21 out of 30 for blacks and 24 out of 30 for whites. Scoring on the OARS Multidimensional Functional Assessment Questionnaire was similar for both groups, indicating mild to moderate overall impairments. Family conferences were held for about a third of the patients in each of the black and white groups. The occurrence of Alzheimer's disease and dementia of all types was the same for both groups. Family burden was a documented problem for about 22% of the black population and about 25% of the white population. Almost 8% of the

Table 1

SUMMARY OF MAJOR DEMOGRAPHIC AND CLINICAL CHARACTERISTICS
OF SAMPLE, BY RACE

CHARACTERISTICS	BLACKS (N=95)		WHITES (N=715)	
Patient Mean Age (in years)	75		76	
Patient Education (in years)	6.0		8.0	
Caregiver Education (in years)	10.5		12	
Patient Income (in thousands of $)	5.5		7.0	
Caregiver Income (in thousands of $)	15.5		21.0	
Caregiver Burden Score (Mean)	26.4		32.0	
Patient MMS Score (Mean)	21/30		24/30	
Patient OARS Score (Means) -Total	17.0		16.5	
Social Resources		3.0		3.0
Economic Resources		3.0		2.5
Mental Health Resources		4.0		4.0
Physical Health		3.0		3.0
ADL		4.0		4.0

	N	%	N	%
Patient Marital Status				
Single	4	4	71	10
Married	27	29	265	38
Widowed	41	44	326	47
Divorced	12	13	25	4
Separated	9	10	5	1
	93*	100	692*	100
Patient Sex				
Male	37	39	182	26
Female	58	61	532	74
	95	100	714*	100
Patient Living Arrangements				
Alone	29	31	221	32
With Others	65	69	470	68
	94*	100	691*	100

*Unknown or missing data.

	Blacks		Whites	
	N	%	N	%
Caregiving Arrangements:				
Self	31	33	320	45
Spouse	19	20	130	18
Sibling	6	06	25	4
Son	5	5	31	5
Daughter	21	22	133	19
Other	13	14	65	9
	95	100	704*	100

	Blacks	Whites
Rate of Family Conferences	34%	33%

Table 1 (Continued)

Rate of Dementia		
Total	46%	46%
Alzheimer's	28%	28%
Multi-Infarct	15%	13%
Other	3%	5%
Rate of Family Burden	22%	25%
Institutionalization Rate	7.9%	9.7%

*Unknown or missing data.

black elderly patients were institutionalized versus 10% of the whites.

The average education for the black group was 6th grade and the average education for the white group was 8th grade. The average income for white patients was less than $7000 per year and the average income for black patients was about $5500 per year. The average income for caregiving families was about $21,000 for white caregivers and about $15,500 for black caregivers.

Table 2 summarizes the results of multiple regression analysis by Beta weights on burden and disposition (i.e., institutionalization) for black and white caregiving groups. The interest was in predicting which set of variables are best predictors for a variety of caregiving groups, especially within the context of Alzheimer's disease. Statistical criteria for variable entry into or removal from the regression equation was as follows: probability of F to enter was 0.05; probability of F to remove was 0.01; the tolerance value was 0.01. Dummy variables were used when appropriate; sociodemographic variables (such as income and education) were included as potential predictors. Although black caregivers experience the problem of burden at the same *rate* as white caregivers, the predictors of burden do differ. Ranked predictors of family burden and disposition according to caregiver race and other subgroups as summarized from this research are listed in Figures 1 and 2.

Multiple regression analyses showed that the best predictors for caretaking burden were patient falls/gait disturbances, dementia, deficits in ADL functioning, living arrangements and lack of social support. This pattern occurred for most patient and caretaking groups. However, there was a differ-

TABLE 2:
BETA WEIGHTS OF PARTIAL REGRESSION COEFFICIENTS
OF SIGNFICIANT VARIABLES FOR BLACK AND WHITE CAREGIVERS

(TOTAL N = 815)

Variables	Family Burden (Whites)	Family Burden (Blacks)	Disposition (Whites)	Disposition (Blacks)
1) Burden			.09	
2) Dementia	.43		.15	
3) Falls		.22	.18	
4) ADL Capacity	.19	.45	.26	
5) Patient Marital Status (Unmarried)		.20		
6) Patient Living Alone	.07			
7) Sensory Loss	.07			
8) Social Support	.09		.07	.24
9) Economic Resources				.31
R^2	.23	.29	.13	.15

ence for black caregivers who experienced less strain in caring for a family member with dementia. Black families were also less likely to institutionalize family members with late-life brain disease. Although the rate of burden for blacks and whites remains the same, black caregivers had burden best predicted by the level of physical ADL capacity, followed by falls, and marital status.

White caregiving families are burdened when the patient has dementia and is unable to perform instrumental daily living tasks such as shopping, preparing meals, handling the finances, taking medicine, and so on. For these tasks, patients need step-by-step reminders to perform them, which require much vigilance on the part of the caregivers. Black caregivers may have fewer problems with the amount of vigilance necessary in caring for Alzheimer's disease patients. Instead, they

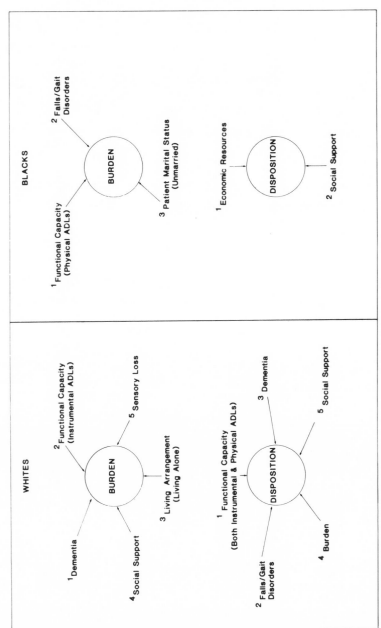

Figure 1

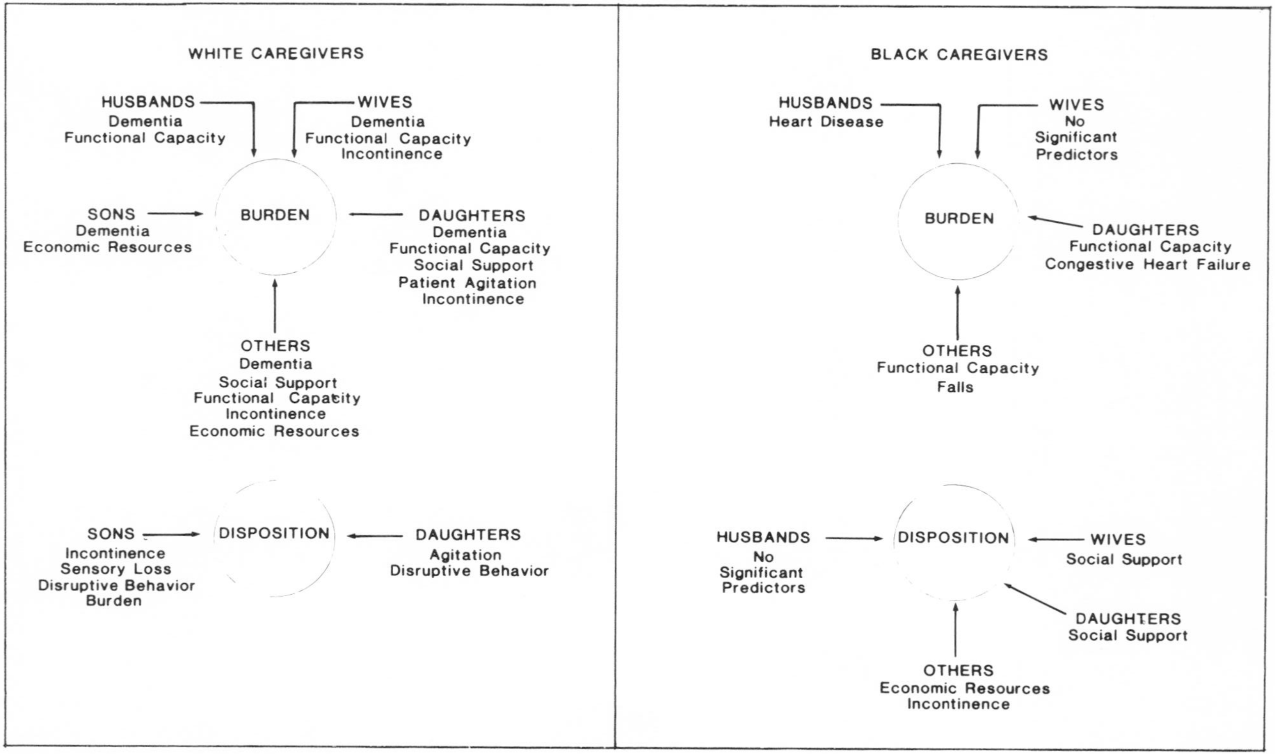

WHITE CAREGIVERS

HUSBANDS
Dementia
Functional Capacity

SONS
Dementia
Economic Resources

WIVES
Dementia
Functional Capacity
Incontinence

DAUGHTERS
Dementia
Functional Capacity
Social Support
Patient Agitation
Incontinence

BURDEN

OTHERS
Dementia
Social Support
Functional Capacity
Incontinence
Economic Resources

SONS
Incontinence
Sensory Loss
Disruptive Behavior
Burden

DAUGHTERS
Agitation
Disruptive Behavior

DISPOSITION

BLACK CAREGIVERS

WIVES
No
Significant
Predictors

HUSBANDS
Heart Disease

DAUGHTERS
Functional Capacity
Congestive Heart Failure

BURDEN

OTHERS
Functional Capacity
Falls

HUSBANDS
No
Significant
Predictors

WIVES
Social Support

DAUGHTERS
Social Support

DISPOSITION

OTHERS
Economic Resources
Incontinence

Figure 2

are burdened by a variety of physical disabilities requiring labor-intensive assistance such as toileting, dressing, bathing, and eating. A t test showed a significant difference in sample means between black and white groups (p = .038) when burden is considered within the context of having dementia. Females of both races experienced more burden than males, with daughters having the higher burden scores than wives.

Also, in this study, the overall institutionalization rate for blacks is only slightly less than for whites (8% for blacks versus 10% for whites); however, blacks institutionalized only 12% of the time when the patient had Alzheimer's disease versus 82% for white caregivers.

The *amount* and the *experience* of stress and strain was quite similar for all caregiving groups, as was the rate of institutionalization. Indeed when the variable of race is entered into multiple regression equations on both burden and institutionalization, its Beta weight is low and insignificant (.010)—and the same is true for both income and education. The study concludes that there is no *essential difference,* based on race, in the experience of family burden as a social problem. Indeed, race, education, and income made little difference in the human response to stress in caring for older, functionally-disabled family members. However, there does seem to be a difference within the interaction of race and the care for an elderly person with Alzheimer's disease; here, there is more strain or felt stress when caregivers are white. When looking at black caregivers as a group, however, Alzheimer's disease offers practically no explanation for the dynamics of family burden or caregiving strain.

These findings, although focusing on possible racial differences, also noted some gender differences, which supports, to a limited extent, the findings of Boutselis and Zarit (1984) and Deimling (1984); both of these studies showed that females experienced more burden than males. This was a consistent finding here as well. Females experienced more burden than males and daughters had a somewhat higher degree of burden than wives. Patient agitation also was a significant predictor of burden for white daughters and of institutionalization for black daughters; this somewhat supports Deimling's (1984) and Wilder's (et al., 1983) studies that showed disruptive behavior was related to increased burden.

Discussion of Research. There are some limiting factors in this study. First, this was not a random sample, and the capability of generalizing to similar settings must be borne out by further research. This is also not a representative sample, but rather a sample compiled from comprehensive geriatric outpatient assessments. The predictive power of particular variables in this research was also constrained by only moderate multiple correlations, by the size of the number of blacks in the sample (N = 95), and by the lack of variability on the type of relationship to the patient, especially among black caregivers (see Table 1). Statistically significant variables still only predict less than 30% of the variance. This study is not a longitudinal design and did not look at a variety of qualitative variables such as prior problem-solving and coping skills, personality traits, role expectations, etc. Finally, although the rate and the experience of burden is similar for both blacks and whites, some differences could be attributed to black families being hesitant in sharing with the professional and mostly white staff.

A major contribution of the Morycz study, however, is that it elaborates on past research concerning the impact of race on caregiving. Although Hanson et al. (1983) found that whites report more socially accepted *answers* regarding filial responsibility norms, in this present study, the actual *behaviors* of black caregivers demonstrated adherence to these norms. This apparent adherence to filial responsibilities among black caregivers has been attributed to socioeconomic status rather than race in past studies (for example, Jackson, 1971; Seebach, 1980). This study does not support the overall importance of socioeconomic differences in caregiving burden; however the availability of economic resources was a critical factor or predictor in the ultimate *disposition* of black patients.

The findings of this research also substantiate Langston's claim (1981), that the black aged have developed and continue to develop natural support networks which enable them to cope with caregiving stress. Furthermore, this current study suggests that the formal human service system should complement the already informal natural network emphasized by both Langston (1981) and Colen (1982). The results here, concerning the experience of burden in black families, add to the existing body of knowledge regarding elasticity and versatility of black family systems (Gibson, 1982; Taylor, 1985). The fact that differences were identified in both white and black families (of the elderly with dementia), relates to earlier studies regarding the varied level of tolerance to caregiving stressors among families (Sheldon, 1982).

II. POSSIBLE CLINICAL IMPLICATIONS FOR PRACTICE

Results of the Morycz study comparing racial differences in the experience of burden suggested that there were specific interventions which are more appropriate for different caregiving groups. Specific interventions have been classified by Fiore et al. (1983) into five overlapping components of support: cognitive guidance, emotional support, socialization, tangible assistance and self-disclosure. Her study correlated the effective use of these components with the severity of depression among caregivers. For purpose of our discussion of this research, we have added differential interventions related to the classifications which are included in Table 3.

Clinical Practice With White Families

For white caregivers, since dementia and instrumental functional capacity were the best predictors of burden in all caregiving groups, caregivers would benefit first from interventions related to *cognitive guidance*. Referring to Table 3, education regarding the nature and prognosis of dementia and interpretation of the medical findings is indicated. The evaluation process should be explained to the family, confirming that all reversible causes have been eliminated. In order to assure the family that the impaired relative's behavior is not willful or intended by the patient to disrupt family life, it is helpful to describe the neurological changes in the brain. If families learn to provide step-by-step instructions, a life-long homemaker would not have to be entirely excluded from meal preparation, thus avoiding the feelings of rejection which may cause behavioral problems. Associating the specific types of cognitive and behavioral problems in the patient with the organic impairment provides a scientific basis for the disease. For instance, explaining that frontal lobe damage can cause a patient to forget the steps involved in preparing a meal will help the caregiver understand the need to provide step-by-step directions.

Cognitive guidance interventions, such as information on available community resources or alternate living arrangements, will help white caregivers develop creative ways to provide home services to their elderly. The helping professional will expand on these interventions and provide *tangible assistance* interventions. Referrals made to the various community resources listed in Part IV of Table 3 will supplement familial efforts to maintain the elderly's optimum independence in instrumental capacity for as long as possible and forestall the experience of burden within the family.

Families would benefit from a realistic assessment of the patient's individual abilities and disabilities and the patient's positive and negative personality characteristics; gaining an understanding of these traits will encourage the most advantageous use of available resources. For example, consider an elderly person who is unsafe around the stove and lives alone. An employed daughter brings in cooked meals every evening, but her mother continues to express feelings of loneliness. Using Meals-on-Wheels would reduce this daily obligation and, more importantly, would introduce a friendly visit from the delivery volunteer into the elderly person's lonely day.

To a lesser degree, the findings of the Morycz study indicated that the elderly person's living alone and the existence of sensory loss added to the white caregiver's feelings of burden (Figure 1). Families need *guidance* to understand the impact of social isolation and the importance of developing social contacts to substitute for lost friends and unavailable family members. In such situations it is especially important to make referrals for tangible services such as Adult Day Care programs.

Along with cognitive guidance, *emotional support* in the form of counseling can identify family strengths and enable the development of expanded and flexible support networks. Efforts to defuse family conflicts and identify obstacles to obtaining or utilizing help will enable filial cooperation and planning for the provision of much needed vigilance to supervise the demented elderly in instrumental functions. Additional interventions that provide *emotional support* can be recommended, such as referral to family support groups.

TABLE 3:
DIFFERENTIAL INTERVENTIONS WITH CAREGIVERS
BY COMPONENT OF SUPPORT

I. Cognitive Guidance: Education & Information Sharing
   - nature of the condition, prognosis and course
   - assessment of individual abilities and disabilities
   - interpretation of comprehensive evaluation
   - community resources
   - alternative living arrangements
   - behavior management techniques
   - environmental manipulation

II. Emotional Support: Individual and Family Counseling
   - reinforcing coping skills
   - strengthening and supplementing family supports
   - defusing family conflicts
   - identifying obstacles to obtaining help
   - empathic listening
   - support groups
   - advocacy

III. Socialization: Respite from Caregiving
   - recreation or leisure activities
   - preservation of privacy

IV. Tangible Assistance: Linkages to Available Resources
    Or Direct Aide
   - financial assistance
   - transportation
   - home health care
   - personal care
   - homemaking services
   - home delivered meals
   - pharmacotherapy
   - companionship or social activities
   - adult daycare
   - short term respite care
   - alternative living arrangements
   - legal services

V. Self-Disclosure: Sharing of Existential Issues
   - guilt
   - anger
   - conflicts (external and internal)
   - ambivalence
   - blame
   - anticipatory grief
   - isolation

*Adapted from Fiore et al., 1983.

Morycz found that an outcome of strain for white caregiving families was seen in changes in their socialization patterns (Morycz et al., 1984). According to the research findings, the outcome of strain on white caregiving families shows that the four most important changes in living patterns relate to *socialization* changes. Helpful interventions in this area would reinforce the need for the white caregiver's recreation, routine respite from caregiving and the development of outside interests (Table 3, Part III).

In a previous Morycz study (1982 and 1985), the desire to institutionalize was slightly higher for white caregivers than black and even more so in white caregiving groups for Alzheimer's patients. Similarly, disposition among white families in the 1984 study was slightly higher than for blacks. The best predictors for institutionalization for whites were the patient's functional capacity, for both instrumental and physical daily living tasks, falls, dementia, burden and social support (Figure 1). For white caregivers of Alzheimer's disease, patient's disposition was best predicted by falls, burden and functional capacity. This pattern seemed consistent for most white subgroups, who were caregivers of Alzheimer's disease patients. The appropriate and timely use of all of the components of support may augment the white family's support system, reduce family burden, prevent injury from falls, and postpone disposition. The recognition of the desire to institutionalize among white caregivers should alert helping professionals to the need for clinical intervention promoting *self-disclosure*. The social worker must provide an opportunity for and even initiate the expressions of guilt, anger, blame and grief. Individual or family counseling sessions will provide an opportunity for *self-disclosure* around the conflicts and ambivalence inherent in caregiving roles and possible anticipatory grief.

Clinical Practice With Black Caregivers

For black families, functional capacity and, more specifically, the physical activities of daily living, best predicted family burden (Figure 1). Apparently, black caregivers in the Morycz study did not experience burden as early as whites. This may relate to the strength of extended family supports among black families, and their ability to share caregiving roles. Also, multigenerational households are said to be more common among black families (Soldo and Myllyluoma, 1983). Black extended family members generally believe if they are sick, they will be cared for (Martin and Martin, 1978). Blacks seem to draw from a more varied pool of informal helpers to cope with stress than do whites and are more versatile in substituting these helpers one for another as they approach old age (Langston, 1981). Therefore, clinical interventions that reinforce these familial and informal supports would be most effective.

Black caregivers in the Morycz study had fewer problems with the constant watching required in giving care to the Alzheimer's disease patient. Instead, they were burdened by tasks necessitating more labor due to the patient's physical disabilities (e.g., toileting, dressing, bathing and eating). Clinical interventions within the *cognitive guidance* component of support should encompass a realistic assessment of the patient's present abilities within the family system and facilitate an understanding of the prognosis. These social work techniques would enable the black family to mobilize its resources and may even prevent future caregiving stress. Black families would benefit from education on what to expect from a patient with dementia, enabling them to cope better in the future, anticipate ways to divide caretaking tasks, and to develop techniques that compensate for impairments.

In comparison to white caregiving groups, the incidence of falls added to the black family's experience of burden but did not tend to be a cause of disposition. This may relate to the fact that blacks have a denser bone mass than whites and are less prone to disabling bone fractures. The impact of falls on the black family's experience of burden suggests that *cognitive guidance* is indicated. For example, black caregivers may benefit from guidance on the extent of supervision required by the elderly patient. Recommendations that black families institute simple environmental changes such as insuring adequate lighting of frequently used hallways and stairs as well as eliminating throw rugs are useful preventive measures. The social worker may also need to advocate for a complete medical work-up to determine if a physical cause for these falls is present.

The third significant predictor of burden among black caregivers relates to the patient's marital status. Since unmarried black females tend to be the poorest of all elderly, a black family may experience increased burden because of financial strain. This indicates the need for tangible assistance and the helping professional should assess the patient's economic resources, advocating the receipt of all financial benefits to which he/she is entitled.

Disruption of household routine was identified in the Morycz study as the most prevalent outcome of strain in black families. Behavioral disruption may include such symptoms of dementia as agitation, sleep disturbance, repetitive questions and angry outbursts. Again, *cognitive guidance* in the form of behavior management techniques or *tangible assistance* interventions such as pharmacotherapy are indicated. *Tangible assistance* from supplemental community resources may also be necessary to conserve the family's energy and maintain mutual goals. Besides direct referral, aggressive advocacy on the black caregiver's behalf is often indicated due to the persistent evidence of institutional victimization (Jackson, 1980) which interferes with elderly blacks and their families' use of available community resources. The social work professional can provide the link for black caregivers to community organizations providing companions, homemaking, personal care and other services as appropriate (Table 3, Part V).

Emotional support interventions are indicated due to the finding that black caregivers reported a change in their relationship to the patient as a second significant outcome of strain. Family conflicts related to these relationship changes may be addressed during family therapy sessions and in support groups. Oftentimes, it is by participating in these support groups that black families may begin to identify obstacles in obtaining help and cope with their changing roles within the family. Thus, black caregivers may become their own advocates on behalf of the patient and their family. Participation in family counseling or support groups also provides an excellent vehicle for *self-disclosure* as caregivers verbalize the conflicts encountered in fulfilling multiple roles, share with other caregivers their sense of isolation, anger and guilt, and anticipate the ultimate loss of the patient.

Black families reported less frequent difficulties with decreased socialization and activities than whites. This difference may manifest the acceptance of caregiving stress as a part of life for black caregivers. Family cohesiveness and the elasticity of the extended family network (Gibson, 1982; Dancy, 1977) may result in black caregivers to perceive little change in their own level of activity and social interaction. However, decreased personal time was identified as significant among outcomes of strain for black caregivers. Interventions which promote *socialization* and routine respite from caregiving are therefore crucial for black caregivers' preservation of privacy.

The desire to institutionalize among black families was reported to a slightly less degree among black families (Morycz, 1982 and 1985). For black caregivers, the desire to institutionalize may be lessened by the elasticity of the family network and the ability of the caregivers to handle multiple roles more comfortably (Colen, 1982). Black caregivers may utilize available extended family supports more often because they are more used to doing so throughout the life cycle; they have more experience at mastering stress (see, for example, Jackson et al., 1977–78). Disability becomes not a burdensome crisis but an accepted part of daily life.

The rate of institutionalization for blacks seemed to relate more to the lack of available environmental resources, i.e., economic and social supports. Many elderly blacks needing extensive personal care are confronted with the problem that their children are working and unable to cease working to care for them due to economic constraints (Jackson, 1980). It is particularly important to ensure that the black elderly patient and his/her family receive all the financial benefits, i.e., *tangible assistance,* to which they are entitled. In addition, the family will be linked to other tangible resources (Part IV, Table 3) in order to conserve the caregiver's energies so they may continue employment.

In spite of these efforts, disposition becomes necessary if no one can stay home to provide extensive personal care. Black families should be supported throughout the disposition process and be given full credit for extending themselves to the maximum. Choosing a long term care facility which will welcome their continued involvement is essential. Obviously, clinical interventions which encompass the *cognitive guidance, emotional support and tangible assistance* components of supports are necessary to educate black families about the resources available, promote effective advocacy and provide the linkages to obtaining services.

Clinical Practice With Caregiving Subgroups

The research referred to in this paper revealed some differences among subgroups in each racial group according to relationship and gender (Figure 2). In all of the white caregiving groups, dementia was the strongest predictor of burden, while functional capacity in instrumental activities was the next predictor in all subgroups, except for sons (See Figure 2). The only other predictor for burden for sons was impaired patient and family economic resources. Social work intervention with white caregiving sons would provide *tangible assistance* in those areas which will supplement household finances. Possibly, those sons in this study experienced similar strain as black caregiving daughters.

Patient agitation was also a significant predictor of burden and the foremost for institutionalization for white daughters. This finding supports other research that found that disruptive behavior is related to increased burden for women (Deimling, 1984). *Tangible assistance* such as assisting the caregiver to request appropriate medication from the physician is a necessary intervention in these cases.

Functional capacity was the greatest predictor of burden for children caring for black elderly. Black husbands, however, reported a health related problem as the greatest predictor and wives appeared to have no predictor. Intervention for these children should focus on those already mentioned in the previous discussion on black caregiving families while black husbands would benefit from *emotional support,* advocating for appropriate medical attention for their own health needs.

A variety of studies have emphasized that the kinship network in black families is quite powerful (Jackson, 1980; Gelfand, 1982), and that black families may rely on extended kin more heavily than white families in times of strain (cf. Wylie, 1971; Haveven, 1980; Devore, 1983). Since predictors of institutionalization in black families are lack of social supports for wives and daughters (Figure 2), it seems that black women need *tangible assistance* to locate support services in the home and for their own *socialization* needs. These formal supports are necessary substitutes when kinship systems become weak or are altogether absent (Luppens et al., 1984).

The findings of the Morycz study, support the findings of Boutselis and Zarit (1984) and Deimling (1984) which showed that females experienced more burden than males. The (former) study also found that daughters in both racial groups had a somewhat higher degree of burden than wives. This may relate to what some studies refer to as role conflicts or role fatigue, which is more common in younger female caregivers (Goldstein et al., 1981; Soldo et al., 1983; Robinson, 1983). *Cognitive guidance,* promoting realistic expectations of the patient's functional capacity and the availability of social support is indicated (Lezak, 1978; Fiore et al., 1983). Women caregivers of both racial groups will benefit from those tangible and community resources which will alleviate strain and promote *socialization.*

Clinical interventions directed towards supporting women in their efforts to find respite while continuing their primary caregiving roles are important. Adult Day Care programs provide the combination of relief from burden and also provide the elderly patient with a much richer and varied experience. Clinicians must also concentrate on *emotional support* interventions such as empathic listening to validate feelings of stress. Then the caregiver can begin to use his/her energy to develop coping skills to plan and take action. Women caregivers often need the strong support of professionals to learn how to expect and obtain cooperation from other family members and from the community.

White families are now dependent on two incomes in most homes and middle-class women of both races are investing themselves into professional careers rather than jobs. It is therefore expected that women will experience greater stress in attempting to fulfill a caregiver role in the future. This warrants targeted efforts towards educating younger generations on ways to develop stronger family and community networks. Learning assertiveness skills will help women set limits on parents who are demanding or who need firm direction and instruction. As women continue to divide themselves between the home and the workplace, role conflicts will increase. Social workers providing family counseling are in the position of guiding women into different role behaviors and assisting in the birth of new role models for their children.

III. CONCLUSIONS

In summary, social workers need to become more sophisticated about the interaction effects of sociodemographic variables relating to caregiving groups. "Ethnic sensitive" social work practice is needed to address the dispositions and behaviors at the intersect of ethnicity and social class (Devore, 1983). Gender sensitivity is also necessary because most long-term care supplied by families is provided by females. Social workers should be encouraged to evaluate caregiving burden with the aid of a brief assessment tool and to differentially intervene in problematic or at-risk situations. This article has attempted to focus upon a few selected variables, most notably race, that provide some insight into possible vulnerable caregiving conditions.

As the mean age of the population rises, as the number of very old increases dramatically, and as social forces continue to complicate family caregiving patterns, the need for intervention to help families care for their elderly will increase. A clinical practice relying on a consistent and organized system, and using these differential but overlapping components of intervention, is needed. These components provide a framework that describes the helping process between the professional and families. In addition, a framework, such as this, identifies those areas of clinical skills which social workers must develop for an effective practice.

REFERENCES

Bengston, V. Ethnicity and aging: problems and issues in current social science inquiry. In Gelfand, D. and Kutzik, A. (Eds.), Ethnicity and aging: Theory, Research, and Policy. Springer Press, New York, 1978.

Boutselis, M., & Zarit S. Burden and distress of dementia caregivers: Effects of gender and relationship. Paper presented at the 37th Annual Meeting of the Gerontological Society of America. San Antonio, Texas, 1984.

Cantor, M. The informal support system of New York's innercity elderly: Is ethnicity a factor? In D. Gelfand and A. Kutzik (Eds.), *Ethnicity and Aging:* Theory, Research, and Policy. New York: Springer, 1979a.

Cantor, M. Life span and social support. In T. Byerts, S. Howell, and L. Pastalan (Eds.), *Environmental Context of Aging.* New York: Garland STP Press, 1979b.

Colen, J.N. Using Natural Helping Networks in Social Service Delivery Systems. In R. C. Manuel (Ed.), *Minority Aging: Sociological and Social Psychological Issues,* Contributions in Ethnic Studies, No. 8. Greenwald Press, Westport, Connecticut, 1982.

Dancy, J. *The Black Elderly.* Institute of Gerontology, Ann Arbor, Michigan, 1977.

Deimling, G. Mental impairment among aged: Effects on spouse and adult-child caregivers. Paper presented at the 37th Annual Meeting of the Gerontological Society of America. San Antonio, Texas, 1984.

Devore, W. Ethnic Reality: The Life Model and Work with Black Families. *Social Casework, 1983, November,* 525–531.

Fiore, J., Becker J., and Coppel, D.B. Social Network Interactions: A Buffer or A Stress. *American Journal of Community Psychology, 1983, 11(4),* 423–439.

Fitting, M. Caregivers for dementia patients: a comparison of men and women. Paper presented at 37th Annual Meeting of the Gerontological Society of America, San Antonio, Texas, 1984.

Gelfand, D. E. *Aging: The Ethnic Factor.* Little Brown and Co., Boston, 1982.

Gibson, R. C. Blacks at middle and late life: resources and coping. *Annals of the American Academy of Political and Social Sciences, 1982, 464,* 79–90.

Goldstein, V., Regenery, G., & Wellin, E. Caretaker Role Fatigue. *Nursing Outlook, 1981, January,* 24–30.

Gonyea, J., and Montgomery, R. Family Caregivers: Who's burdened. Paper presented at the 37th Annual Meeting of the Gerontological Society of America. San Antonio, Texas, 1984.

Hanson, S. L., Sauer, W. J., & Seebach, W. C. Racial and Cohort Variations in Filial Responsibility Norms. *Gerontologist, 1983, 23(6),* 626–631.

Haveven, T. Main themes of the mini-conferences from a historical perspective. In the Social Welfare Forum, 1979: Proceedings from the 106th Annual Forum of the National Conference on Social Welfare. Columbia University Press, New York, 1980.

Henderson, J. Creating culturally relevant Alzheimer's support groups for racial and ethnic minorities. Symposium presented at the 37th Annual Meeting of the Gerontological Society of America.

Jackson, J. J. *Minorities and Aging.* Wadsworth Publishing Company, Belmont, California, 1980.

Jackson, J. J. Negro Aged: Toward Needed Research in Social Gerontology. *Gerontologist, 1971, 11,* 52–57.

Jackson, J., Bacon, J., & Peterson, J. Life satisfaction among black urban elderly. *International Journal of Aging and Human Development, 1977–78, 8,* 169–180.

Langston, E. J. Kith and Kin: Natural Support Systems. In S. E. Percil (Ed.), *Minority Aging: Policy Issues for the 80s.* Companile Press, San Diego, California, 1981.

Lezak, M. Living with the Characterologically Altered Brain Injured Patient. *Journal of Clinical Psychiatry, 1978, 39,* 592–598.

Luppens, J., Harel, Z. and Wyatt, J. Predictors of Home Based Long-Term Care Services. Paper presented at the 37th Annual Meeting of the Gerontological Society of America, San Antonio, Texas, 1984.

Martin, E. and Martin, J. *The Black Extended Family.* University of Chicago Press, Chicago, 1978.

Morycz, R. Family Burden and Outpatients with Alzheimer's Disease. Doctoral Dissertation: University of Pittsburgh School of Social Work, 1982. Ann Arbor, Michigan: University Microfilms, 1982.

Morycz, R. Caregiving strain and the desire to institutionalize family members with Alzheimer's disease: Possible predictors and model development. *Research on Aging, 1985, 7,* 329–361.

Morycz, R., Malloy, J., and Bozich, M. Family Burden as a Social Problem in a Geriatric Ambulatory Care Center: Possible Racial Differences. Paper presented at the 37th Annual Meeting of the Gerontological Society of America, San Antonio, Texas, 1984.

Niederche, G., et al. Measuring family system characteristics in families caring for dementia patients. Paper presented at the 35th Annual Meeting of the Gerontological Society of America, Boston, 1982.

Ory, M. G. et al. Families informal supports and Alzheimer's disease. Current research and future agendas. Working document of work group on families, informal supports, and Alzheimer's disease of the Department of Health and Human Services. Taskforce on Alzheimer's Disease, 1984.

Robinson, B. C. Validation of a Caregiver Strain Index. *Journal of Gerontology,* 1983, *38(3),* 344–348.

Schultz, R., & Rau, M. T. Social Support through the Life Course. In S. Cohen and C. L. Syme (Eds.), *Social Support and Health.* Academic Press, New York, 1985. In press.

Seebach, W. C. Filial Responsibility among Aged Parents: a racial comparison. *Journal of Minority Aging,* 1980, *5(2–4),* 286–292.

Shanas, E. The Family as a Social Support System in Old Age. *Gerontologist,* 1979, *19,* 169–183.

Sheldon, F. Supporting the Supporters: Working With the Relatives of Patients with Dementia. *Age and Ageing,* 1982, *11,* 184–188.

Soldo, B. and Myllyluoma, J. Caregivers who Live with Dependent Elderly. *Gerontologist,* 1983, *23(6),* 605–611.

Taylor, R. The extended family as a source of support to elderly blacks. *Gerontologist,* 1985, *25,* 488–495.

Todd, P., Zarit, J., and Zarit, S. Differences over time between men and women caregivers. Paper presented at 37th Annual Meeting of the Gerontological Society of America, San Antonio, Texas, 1984.

Wilder, D., Teresi, J., and Bennett, R. Family Burden and Dementia, *Advances in Neurology,* 1983, 239–251.

Wylie, F. M. Attitudes Toward Aging and the Aged Among Black Americans: Some Historical Perspectives. *Aging and Human Development,* 1971, *2,* 66–70.

Zarit, S., Reever, K., & Back-Peterson, J. Relatives of the impaired elderly: Correlates of feelings of burden. *Gerontologist,* 1980, *20,* 649–655.

WORLD OF PRACTICE

Mother's Coming Home Today

Frances D. Thurston, MSW

ABSTRACT. Through use of hypothetical case material, this paper explores the social and emotional impact of discharge planning on an older patient, who has been in the hospital, and on her family. Three major areas are examined: mobilizing families through the crisis of illness; the need for early discharge planning to determine options and meet the federal-state regulations; and the potential for burn-out which exists in the discharge planner. The case material focuses on how a family experiences illness and responds to the discharge planning process.

Mother's coming home today. She's been in the hospital. Trouble is, she's not ready, and I'm not ready, but there's nothing we can do about it. What's wrong with her? Well, let's put it this way: When you're 83 it seems like everything happens at once. Mother's had diabetes and high blood pressure for a long time now. Sometimes she has trouble with her kidneys, too. She's been on all kinds of medicine. She called me that Saturday morning and told me she had fallen down (one of her "sinking spells" she called it). I got over there as fast as I could—had to take a cab because the kids had the car again—and that whole morning was a nightmare. She was

Mrs. Frances D. Thurston, MSW, is the Social Work Coordinator of the Geriatric Service at New York Hospital-Cornell Medical Center, Westchester Division, White Plains, New York, and is a Lecturer in Social Work, Department of Psychiatry, Cornell Medical Center.

terribly confused and had wet herself. By the time I got the doctor and the ambulance and got her cleaned up, it seemed like half the day had gone by. We arrived at the hospital (where naturally I couldn't find her Medicare card, there was such a jumble in her purse), and it seemed like that emergency room was packed solid with crying children. It was some scene. Mother was confused and scared. It felt like an eternity before the doctor got to us and I finished filling in all those forms and answering questions. Wouldn't you know, that was the day Joe and I had planned to go to the country. Of course we never did get there.

So she's been in the hospital and now she's coming home. The doctor says among other things she had a small stroke, her diabetes was out of control, and something was wrong with her kidneys. Poor soul, she's had a rough time of it and lots of tests. She's been on intravenous and they had to change her insulin, and they did some kind of kidney procedure that I still don't understand, but to be honest with you, I don't think she's that well yet. The government does, though.

I received a letter from the hospital (the one the social worker had warned me about) telling me about Mother's assigned length of stay and that she'd have to be discharged as soon as her "level of care" wasn't "acute" anymore. So I was warned. And I did get notified when Mother would have to be discharged. It's almost like the government doesn't think it's important that an old lady still wets herself and, like I said, she doesn't seem all that well to me yet. She still gets confused. Yesterday she called me by my sister's name, and she gets the kids terribly mixed up when they visit her. Joe says we'll have to bring her home to our house. He doesn't think she's in any shape to go back to her apartment. To do that I'm going to have to double the girls up in one bedroom. We already have Joe's mother living with us since his Dad died.

I knew about bed utilization and assigned lengths of stay. I knew it, but I didn't believe it. Right after Mother was admitted, the social worker called and then Joe and I went to that family meeting where they explained federal regulations and early discharge planning. The trouble is, you hear these things, but they don't mean anything to you when you're worrying about your parent being sick. Who can think about discharge when your mother's got tubes sticking out of her every which way? Then it happens. Like I say, I don't think she's ready, and I know I'm not.

You ask: What's the big problem? Everybody has to come home from a hospital some time. It's just that I think Mother doesn't seem all that well yet. Dr. Stone says give it time, let her get her strength back, but somehow I feel uneasy because she's just not anywhere near herself yet.

By last week when I saw how slow things were going, I thought we'd have Mother go to St. Agnes Nursing home for a little while, just until she got her strength back. Mother used to do volunteer work at St. Agnes and she knows all the sisters there. I read in the Medicare handbook about the 100 days of convalescent care when you leave the hospital, and it just seemed that would be the ideal solution, until I talked to Miss Norman, the social worker. She said it was "very unlikely" that Medicare would pay for Mother's stay in a nursing home because her care would most likely be "custodial" and not "skilled." It's either private funds or Medicaid. Besides, she says, St. Agnes has a six-month waiting list. Well, I re-read the handbook and there it was, all that confusing jargon about "custodial" care with a lot of "only if" this and "only if" thats. Naturally, I didn't pay any attention to all those clauses the first time I read them.

Which brings me to another problem: the way I feel about the doctor and the social worker. They've been so good to me, and to Mother, but now that this length of stay cut-off they kept talking about is here, it seems they can't help us anymore. I know they warned me about making early discharge plans. But Mother's condition seemed so uncertain. One day it was good. The next day she was weak and confused, or running a temperature, or throwing up. It seems like it's just gone from one thing to another. To me, Mother's not all that well. But now there's been a "determination" that Mother's no longer "acute" and that we have to make "alternate plans." I'd like to see what "alternate plans" Dr. Stone and Miss Norman would make if it were their mother. It's funny how you can like two people so much, but hate them at the same time. I know they didn't make those regulations, and they've been really good to me. But all I know is I feel very upset now, and it's easier to be angry at them than some faceless people I'll never see sitting in Washington.

Since Medicare doesn't pay for the nursing home, Miss Norman suggested looking into Medicaid. When I called they couldn't even give me an appointment in less than two weeks. Besides I found that Mother would have to "spend down" her savings. When Dad died he left her a little money, so Mother has a few thousand in the bank. She's always looked to that "rainy day," though I know she wanted to use it for those little extras when the kids go off to college. Under Medicaid Mother would be allowed to keep a certain amount exempt, but the rest of her savings would have to be spent before she would be eligible for medical assistance. So to get her in a nursing home just until she's stronger, she'd have to pretty much wipe out her savings the way convalescent care costs today.

Next I talked to the home care nurses. Again Mother's needs aren't skilled enough to pay for a part-time health aide. Help with bathing, dressing, shopping, cooking and household chores are all the things Medicare calls "custodial." If Mother returns to her apartment right now, I know she'd need someone round-the-clock while she's still so confused and weak, and that's going to cost plenty. Again, this pretty much takes care of her savings. Everything Dad worked so hard to put away for the two of them.

So it all comes back to Joe and me. The girls are just going to have to double up. With college right around the corner, I'm working now. That means hiring someone for eight hours. At what it costs an hour, any way you look at it, Mother's "rainy day" fund is going to be pretty slim.

At least Mother's got Joe and me to do some worrying for her. What I wonder is: how do old people get along when they don't have any family left? With all the help Miss Norman's given me, it seems like I've still had to make a hundred phone calls. I've learned a lot about how much red tape there is in this world with all the Medicare and Medicaid regulations you have to pick your way through. I can't tell you how many times I've been put on hold, and how many hours I've spent trying to get through to the Social Security Office. It's not their fault, I know they're awfully busy, but how do single old people manage this on their own? I couldn't believe the documentation I'd have to bring in to apply for Medicaid. I know Medicaid isn't a charity. But still, just getting your checks and bankbooks and life insurance and rent receipts and proof of age and residence must be rough if you don't have anybody to help you. What if your mother's a bit confused, or your father's too sick to tell you where to look for his papers and bankbooks? In Mother's case, she doesn't have the required birth certificate. When she was born in the 1890's in Mississippi, they didn't keep birth records. So if we ever have to apply to Medicaid, I'll have to locate some other kinds of proof of her age.

I don't mean to sound bitter or ungrateful. It's just that it's not easy to be old and sick, and it bothers me to see how little choice there is for an older person when he's ready to leave the hospital. If you need to go to a nursing home, and you live near a large city in the Northeast like we do, your private costs are going to run a couple of thousand dollars a month, which is pretty quick "spend down" for the average person. But then once you've spent down, how do you ever go home again? If you try to recuperate at home, Medicare won't pay for full-time services, medications, or delivery of meals to your home. And if Mother were on Medicaid, the most they usually pay for a homemaker is 8 to 10 hours a day. What's an old person supposed to do for those other 14 hours? What happens if the homemaker gets sick and doesn't show up one day? Or there's a snow storm? Or what if the old person falls down at night while going to the bathroom? I don't know. Maybe I worry too much, but it seems to me between Title-this and Title-that, and what's available for old people, we don't provide many incentives to stay at home.

For us the decision's all made and Mother's coming home today. We've got the homemaker lined up while I'm at work. It's going to be expensive, but somehow we'll manage. The girls have been good sports about sharing a room. You know teenagers and their need for privacy, especially Ellen and all the music she listens to. Mother's Social Security checks will maintain her apartment, and when she feels stronger she'll have her own place to go back to. It's going to be hard, but somehow I know we'll make out.

But as I've said, what I keep thinking about, is how old people manage when they don't have anyone to help them out. I remember asking Miss Norman that very question. What happens to people when they're all alone? Miss Norman said that was her nightmare. She said sometimes she literally gets a stomach ache trying to cut through all the red tape to get services for these old people who have no one. She told me about people who had to be institutionalized because they didn't have any better alternative. Not that there aren't some excellent nursing homes. But I started thinking about it and I wondered what it would be like to share a room with someone I'd never known before. To have my kids visit me in a strange place. I wondered how I would feel if I were on Medicaid and my "allowance" wouldn't let me buy stockings this month, or a toy for a grandchild. I thought about these things and I realized that someday I, too, would be old and I wondered how good my alternatives would be. We've had a rough time these last few weeks with Mother, but the more I think about it, the more I realize that we're among the lucky ones. Mother's coming home today. At least she has a home, and she has us. I can't help wondering about those others who don't.

DISCUSSION

This case represents a situation common to any medical or psychiatric hospital in the United States admitting elderly patients. It could be described as an example of a patient at moderate risk. This 83 year-old woman, in a convalescent phase and still in need of ongoing care, does not have a seriously debilitating illness. With proper supports, her chances for recovery are quite good. Her family is warmly involved (despite some conflict on the part of her daughter), and she has access to private funds, allowing her some choice in the purchase of health services. On a scale of 1 to 10, her family would rank about 4 in terms of crisis and stress. But even in this most "ordinary" of discharge situations, the potential for poor outcome exists.

All hospitals today are mandated to shorten their length of stay. The older patient, often with a multiplicity of chronic disorders, often falls out of assigned lengths of stay. Despite repeated attempts to educate people about alternate levels of care, families are generally so involved in the crisis of an older relative's illness that they are literally unable to hear us when we talk about the necessity of early discharge planning. Often hospitalization of the elderly is the final step in a series of ongoing and mounting crises. In situations where there is a life-threatening or severely disabling illness, the family has to first deal with its natural grief before mobilizing itself for action. Frequently this is where families get stuck. It's almost impossible to think about discharge, assigned lengths of stay, and termination of insurance benefits when a family member is in a coma, or on life-support aids. It's equally difficult to make plans, as in this more "ordinary" situation, when the patient's medical status fluctuates from day to day and families are uncertain of what can be considered a consistent baseline.

In addition to the crisis of illness and the family's ability to cope, we are constantly operating within a framework of immutable realities. These realities involve planning for institutional or home-health care, applying for financial aid, gathering the necessary, but time-consuming, documentation, and exploring the availability of community supports.

Another risk factor in discharge planning is the effect of "immutable realities" on social workers, or other health professionals, who are constantly, intimately involved in the process. The psychologist, Christina Maslach, one of the early researchers on "burn-out," described that emotional exhaustion where helping professionals lose their creativity, commitment, and enthusiasm because of unending demands on their energy, strength, and resources. Maslach found that what was common to people who "burn out" was that hour after hour, day after day, they were intimately involved in the psychological, social and physical problems of troubled human beings. Eventually this close, continuous contact, where the success level is only modest, can lead to psychological detachment, emotional exhaustion, or discouragement and cynicism.[3]

Too often in the drudgery which has become part of discharge planning—the mandated paperwork, the unending telephone calls, the lack of good choices, the misery of many of the patients and families we work with, the suspicion at times that we have become enforcers rather than enablers—all of this can lead to our own crisis of soul.

Too often we see the potential for institutionalization that exists in the discharge of too many hospitalized elderly people. Seldom are there easy choices. If the patient in our hypothetical case had not had an involved family, if she had not had private funds, if she had not had a place to return to, there might have been a totally different outcome to her discharge. Had she been a little sicker and had no choice other than a nursing facility, she might have gotten caught in the Medicaid dilemma that so often haunts the older person. People needing nursing home care must deplete their financial resources before they are eligible for Medicaid assistance. But eventually if their health improves enough to leave the facility, where can they go? Once their resources are gone and their home and furnishings have been given up, the option of leaving the nursing institution becomes an unrealistic one.

As long as the federal government chooses a policy that links long-term and home-health care almost exclusively to private pay or the Medicaid system, and as long as we provide few alternatives for community-based services at affordable prices, long-term care in institutions will remain the primary alternative for the elderly.

As long as we continue to differentiate, through federal policy, between "skilled" and "custodial" care, we are going to continue to promulgate a system that promotes dependency and institutionalization. In our example, if this 83 year-old had had the choice of either reimbursed short-term convalescence in a nursing facility, or adequate reimbursed home-care services, both she and her family might have made what was, for them, more optimal plans. In the long run, since so many people end up permanently institutionalized at enormous expense to the taxpayer, these choices would also be cost-effective. Our hypothetical patient was a relatively fortunate patient with a good support system, but her family still had to make choices that weren't entirely optimal.

Others are not so lucky. As Medicaid recipients, few people are allowed 24-hour at-home services, often so critical in that period immediately following hospitalization—hospitalizations under the DRGs that are becoming increasingly short. In terms of scarce nursing home beds, Medicaid recipients have almost no choices. In New York State, for example, there are stringent regulations for the institutional placement of Medicaid patients. Acute bed shortages mandate that social workers be "aggressive" in their search. Patients enter the long-term care system via a scored nursing assessment which assigns "points" for categories of nursing care, functional ability, and mental status. (Among other things, blindness is scored only 2 "points," while someone needing help in dressing receives a score of 80). The aggregate score determines the level of care a patient needs, and this serves as the patient's entry into the long-term care system. Literally hundreds of these forms are sent out from New York area hospitals, in numbers that increase weekly for each waiting patient. These mailings are followed by hundreds of weekly telephone calls, along with mandated medical chart documentation as to one's "activities" in efforts to discharge a patient. Family and patient preference is a nonexistent factor in this search, since regulations state that the first available bed, out of however many applied for, must be taken within 24 hours. This is a less than humane system—in truth a cynical game of chance—and one that often causes real hardship for families who are sometimes forced to travel long distances to areas where there is little direct transportation. The greatest hardship is that befalling couples separated for the first time in perhaps forty, fifty, sixty years of marriage.

In a system like this (and undoubtedly each state has its own particular Medicaid regulations) the social worker comes to put value on things like private savings to the exclusion of human needs and choice. There is seldom difficulty in finding placement of choice for patients with sufficient money. For the social worker who has been engaged in intensive counseling and planning, and who has developed a relationship of trust with clients, it's difficult to change roles and inform people of length-of-stay termination and the fact that choice in a nursing home is not going to be theirs. This is what is meant about crisis of soul. This is where the social worker begins to feel less like a helping professional and more like an "enforcer."

Service provision for the elderly is often fragmented so that as Claude Pepper, the venerable Representative from Florida, said in a speech to Congress:

> . . . when an older person has a need for a particular service, for example in-home health services, where can he turn for help? The answer, unfortunately, is 'it all

depends.' Home health and supportive services are provided under Medicare, Medicaid, and the social services program under Title XX . . . the Public Health Service Act . . . the Older Americans Act . . . ACTION . . . the Older Americans Community Service Employment program, Senior Opportunities and Services under the Community Services Act, and other statutes. All of this adds up to a bewildering maze of programs and regulations that is a nightmare for the elderly person trying to find his or her way through it. (p. 76)[1]

CONCLUSION

To be elderly and in a hospital is to be at some risk at time of discharge. Several factors influence an older person's exit from the hospital.

The first factor has to do with how quickly and early the worker can move in to begin future discharge planning. In this age of careful cost accounting and assigned lengths of stay, discharge planners don't have much time for the examination of alternatives to particular actions. In what ought to be one of three simple choices, returning to one's home, going to live with a friend or relative, or entering a long-term care facility, the seeds of failure can be present. Thus, mobilizing families, dealing with the immediacy of crisis, helping people to set priorities, and exploring realistic alternatives are all part of that first critical factor.

The second factor is another form of mobilization, or what Claude Pepper describes as helping people through the "bewildering maze." If someone is going to need Medicaid assistance, we have to ensure that the application is started. If an old gentleman needs homemaking assistance, this has to be arranged. The same is true of meals, home care equipment, the visiting nurse, transportation to the doctor or the day care center, and a host of necessary services. Who will provide them? How are they to be paid for?

The third factor is that discharge planners have to be absolutely accurate in their understanding of Medicare's definition of "skilled" and "custodial" services. Within this distinction lies the determination of what will be paid for and what will not. If we cannot distinguish between the two, we lead people to make choices that cannot be fulfilled.

And last is our own factor as professionals: the problem of burn-out. The less effective we feel as enablers, the more we experience ourselves as enforcers, the more we erode our sense of enthusiasm, our creativity, our energy, and our ability to be helpful to those who depend on us for effective discharge plans. Each of us needs to search for creative possibilities, to learn all we can about community resources, to network with others who serve the elderly, so that we don't get bogged down with disenchantment and pessimism about possibilities for the elderly.

There are many creative long-term care programs which have been developed in this country. Respite care, day centers, family support groups, long-term home health programs are examples of just a few. They are community-based, highly supportive to family caregivers, and can often prevent unnecessary institutionalization.

But despite proliferation of good, sensible community supports, it continues to be hard to maintain optimism in this period of cost containment and sometimes premature discharges of Medicare patients. Federal policy is still linked to a system tying home-health and institutional care almost exclusively to Medicaid. As Kaufman points out, "this approach has resulted in an almost exclusive emphasis on institutionalization as the means of obtaining long-term care services for aged persons whose families are unable or unwilling to provide this care. Such a policy has severe negative economic and social consequences . . ."[2]

The hypothetical case in this article could be any one of our parents or grandparents. It is the same person we work with daily in medical and psychiatric settings. There are no easy solutions, but Kaufman again comes closest to some kind of an answer when he says that the "federal government must address itself to the task of developing a comprehensive policy toward the entire issue of long-term care for the aged."[2]

Until we can help bring about fundamental changes in what our society offers for older people, we will continue to agonize how best to plan hospital discharges in the face of federal regulations, cost containment, and assigned lengths of stay. The Gray Panthers describe it well:

when persons are old . . . they are seen as problems to society, rather than as persons experiencing problems created by society. The natural result . . . is to suggest ways in which older people need to adjust to society, rather than how society may be changed to adjust to the needs of older people." (p. 226)[1]

It would seem that our legacy, and our challenge as health care professionals, is to promote changes in a system that continues to view its older members as problems to society. Only then will we advance discharge planning into a process that is both realistic and humane.

REFERENCE NOTES

1. Estes, Carroll L. *The Aging Enterprise,* Jossey-Bass Publishers, San Francisco, 1979.
2. Kaufman, Allan, "Social Policy and Long-Term Care of the Aged," *Social Work,* Vol. 25, No. 2, March 1980.
3. Maslach, Christina, "Burn-Out Syndrome: A Social Psychological Analysis." Paper presented at the Annual Convention of the American Psychological Association, San Francisco, August 1977.

REFERENCES

Christ, Winifred "Factors Delaying Discharge of Psychiatric Patients" *Health and Social Work,* Summer 1984, 178–187.
Memoranda from New York State Department of Health; Empire State Medical, Scientific and Educational Foundation, Inc.; Hospital Association of New York State; Medicare Bulletins, Department of Health, Education and Welfare, Washington, D.C.
Horn, S.D., Bulkley, G., Sharkey, P.D., Chambers, A.F., Horn, R., Schramm, C.J. "Interhospital Differences in Severity of Illness: Problems for Prospective Payment Based on Diagnostic-Related Groups (DRGs)" *New England Journal of Medicine,* July 4, 1985.

Groups With Families of Elderly Long-Term Care Residents: Building Social Support Networks

Ellie Brubaker, PhD, ACSW
Ann Ward Schiefer

ABSTRACT. This article examines a group which was developed for children of elderly long-term care residents. The group functioned to provide emotional and social support for family group members. A long range goal of the group was the development of a support network available to families of incoming residents. The group's composition, format and leadership are discussed. Findings reveal that group involvement facilitated family members in their relationship to their resident-relatives, in their acceptance of long-term care for their relatives and in their involvement in a social support system for other family members.

The idea that families can benefit from services is not a new one. Family members of elderly clients have often been incorporated into the "client system." It is also possible for both families and elderly residents to gain from the involvement in the "service system." It has been suggested that for elderly living within the community setting, the involvement of both relatives and professional service providers can contribute to the well-being of the elderly (Strieb, 1972; Blenkner, 1965; Sussman, 1977). In the same way, relatives and professionals can work together within a long-term care setting to develop and provide services. Family members can provide support for one another as well as for their older relatives. When this is successfully accomplished, the older resident's and the family's adjustment to the long-term care situation is facilitated.

Ellie Brubaker is at Miami University, Oxford, Ohio; and Ann Ward Schiefer is with Oxford View Nursing Center, Oxford, Ohio.

167

For residents of long-term care facilities, relationships with family members are important. The research literature indicates that elderly persons in long-term care maintain continued, regular contact with their families (Brubaker and Brubaker, 1984). As a result, staff employed by long-term care facilities frequently find themselves in the position of working with the families of residents. Success of the family-staff relationship may influence the adjustment of the residents to the facility. If family members are anxious concerning their older relative's placement, these feelings will likely be translated to the resident. It may be the resident him/herself who exhibits symptoms of the family's feelings to the staff. Conversely, both residents and staff benefit from the positive experiences of family members (Cohen, 1983). *This article describes a program established to lessen the anxiety of family members of elderly long-term care residents.* The program focused to *provide services* to family members with the long-term goal of having families facilitate one another through the *development of an informal support network.*

Various strategies can be utilized to encourage family participation with service providers within a long-term care setting. Numerof (1983:57) suggests that institutional programs for the elderly need to "build bridges between the nursing home and the outside home." Involving relatives as participants in a group is one strategy for including family members in the older resident's care. Group work with families can function to enable relatives to feel comfortable with the facility so that they can enact supportive behavior with their own relative-residents and with other families. Groups also allow families to share experiences with other members within a structured environment. The literature points to the success of groups in enabling relatives of the elderly to deal with personal issues (Hartford and Parsons, 1982).

THE SETTING

In one long-term care facility, a group for family members was organized in order to provide better services for family members and, indirectly, for residents. The social service staff of the nursing facility, a 79 bed skilled care facility, had two objectives. These included: (1) to enable participants to gain support from other group members; and (2) to encourage participants to develop supportive relationships with family members not involved in the group. The second objective reflects the belief that family members can develop support networks which enhance the adjustment of other residents' relatives, with guidance from long-term social service professionals.

DEVELOPMENT OF THE GROUP

With the above objectives in mind, resident's records were reviewed to determine which family members could: (1) benefit from support provided through a group setting, (2) provide support to group members and (3) following the group experience be available to family members of other residents. Eight individuals were chosen and letters were sent to each outlining the reason for initiating the group and requesting their participation. The letters were followed by a telephone call, inquiring whether the family members would be willing to participate. Six individuals who had been contacted agreed to become involved in the group.

The individuals who were chosen had a number of commonalities. All were women, all visited their resident-relative regularly, all were daughters whose resident-relative was a mother and all currently or in the past had difficulties with the dependency involved in their relationships with their mother. Although the situations of the group participants had similarities, each member had different personal characteristics and differing responses to their mother's situations. The similarity of situations provided a basis for group discussions which served to enhance participation, while the differences in personalities allowed for participants to balance one another and grow from contact with the strengths of others. In addition, participants had often found solutions to problems which other members had not explored. Getzel (1983) notes that these experiences can be shared in group settings.

The group was co-led by the facility's social service director and a social worker who was not a full-time employee of the facility. In addition to the advantage of stability provided by co-leadership of two professionals (Szafranski, 1984), the employment status of the leaders was relevant. For participants, their prior relationship with the social service director enabled them to feel more comfortable in the group, while the leadership of the social worker facilitated expression of concerns about the facility.

The group was planned for six one-hour sessions. Prior to the first session, each group member was apprised of the goals of the group and format was discussed. Each of the members already had a relationship with the social service director, but none had previously met the social worker involved in co-leading the group. Although the group members had seen one another on occasion when visiting their mother, they were not closely acquainted. In one case, two of the members' mothers were roommates, but the daughters had not spent significant time talking with one another prior to the beginning of the group.

GROUP FORMAT

The group began by focusing on the objectives of providing support to group members and developing relationships between the group members which could continue after the termination of the group. Consequently, the first group session was primarily directed toward acquainting members with one another, reclarifying group goals and developing trusting relationships between the group leaders and group members. In the first session, the leaders explained that the participants' statements would be kept confidential from other staff and residents at the facility.

In order to discuss topics which would allow group members to share experiences and provide support for one another, a focus was placed on stresses which they experienced in relation to their mothers' placements. The second, third and fourth sessions dealt with issues related to having a mother placed in the facility. Primary emphasis was given to their relationships with their mothers and their families. The conflict which sometimes resulted from trying to meet the emotional needs of a number of people close to them was discussed. Participants were encouraged to share similar experiences. They discovered that they could verbally provide information which would be helpful to one another and could validate the importance of the feelings of other group members.

At the time of the fifth session, discussion was opened to concerns the residents had about the facility itself. The co-leaders did not approach this topic until the fifth session, until trust in the group participants and leaders was clearly established. In addition, by this time, the participants recognized that they were viewed as an integral part of the facility and consequently, their comments were constructive and responsible. This issue was suggested for discussion to enable group members to present ideas for ways in which the facility could better serve them. When families view the facility as an enabling institution rather than as a problem, residents are more likely to hold this view as well. Also, ideas developed from the discussion which allowed participants to view themselves as able to work *with* the facility.

The final session was used to evaluate the group experience and to reemphasize the potential of the group members in relation to the facility. Specifically, the issue of group members becoming involved as part of a support network to other families was discussed. This included their continuing support for one another and developing themselves as resources for families of other residents. It was suggested that the social servce director would coordinate the development of an informal support network for families, providing family members new to the facility with names and telephone numbers of willing group members.

Each session involved structured exercises as well as open-ended discussions. Often the exercises provided the impetus for discussion. Various resources exist to provide structure for groups. For the group described, a manual for working with family members provided some of the exercises (Springer and Brubaker, 1984).

OUTCOMES OF THE GROUP

The two objectives for the group, developed prior to the group's establishment, were for group members to become supportive of one another and to branch out in order to provide support for other residents' families. The first objective was accomplished during the meetings. Group members stated that they found themselves feeling "less alone" in their situations. They indicated throughout the meetings that it was helpful for them to hear that others were going through situations similar to theirs. When one group member discussed how her mother's behavior often contributed to her feelings of guilt, several other members nodded and another said, "You, too? I though I was the only person who ever felt that way!"

At another time, when discussing the conflict which they felt when trying to meet their mother's emotional needs *and* their children's and husband's needs, one member expressed feelings of anger toward her husband. Another member indicated that she occasionally had similar feelings. The members discussed the possiblity that husbands occasionally were the only individuals on whom they could take out their frustrations. It was helpful to realize that because their husbands were often the recipients of their frustrations, they were not necessarily the cause. This discovery could also be applied to their relationship with the long-term care facility. At times, *the facility—and staff—may be the "safest" target for expressing frustration, but perhaps not the reason for their anger.*

For one group member, hearing from the daughter (another group member) of her mother's roommate that her mother functioned happily in her absence was a relief. Although she had been told this by staff, hearing this from a nonstaff member was especially reassuring to her. Families can provide information to one another that staff members may not know about or may not be trusted to give.

As indicated above, during the final session the members evaluated the group experience. They stated that they had found the group helpful in the following ways:

1. *Knowing that others shared similar experiences helped them to feel less alone.* Some of the members had felt that they were doing something wrong because they became so easily overwhelmed. Discovering that their experience was "normal" for someone in their situation was helpful.

2. *Recognizing that the facility was concerned about their well-being was reassuring to them.* Some of the concerns which they had brought up about the facility had been handled confidentially by the social service director.
3. Some of the group members were in different stages of their relationships with their mothers. *Those members who had worked out a more satisfactory, less dependent relationship were able to serve as models for those who had not. In addition, this provided hope that problems could be worked through.*

Following the group's termination, group members continued to see one another when visiting their mothers. This too has been a source of help.

Although the group proved helpful to most of the participants, not all benefited equally. One member, who was unable to attend consistently, was very concerned about her mother. For her, either the lack of regular group attendance or the extent of her concern, prevented her from receiving the support she needed. Individual meetings with the social service director would likely have been more helpful. Extremely anxious family members have the potential to dominate the group and may be unable to appropriately utilize support provided by others in the group setting.

The second objective, for the group members to provide support for other resident's families, is still being accomplished. At the final session, all the participants who attended agreed to become involved in this. Because of the help they received, they are aware of the kinds of support which is most beneficial to others. New residents' families have been contacted by group members and have found this to be helpful. Specifically, the families benefit from learning about the experiences of others who have relative-residents in the facility and from an awareness that someone with similar experiences is available to them if needed. This does not in any way replace the work of the social service director, but supplements his/her work. This support of someone who is not a staff member and who has gone through a similar experience is something which cannot be duplicated by an employee of the facility.

SUMMARY AND CONCLUSIONS

This article describes a project in which a group was established for family members of long-term care residents. The dual purpose of the group was to provide support for group members and to develop, through the group members, a support network for the families of incoming residents. The development, format and outcomes of the group are discussed. The choice of members, leaders and group structure contributed to the achievement of the group's goals. For participants, the group experience provided support, increased acceptance of their situation and developed their ability to serve other families involved with the long-term care facility.

It was found that family members can personally benefit from support provided by their cohorts within a group setting. The relationship between family members and the long-term care facility was strengthened through the use of the group. Specifically, co-leadership by the facility's social service director and an independent social worker contributed to a non-threatening environment in which family members could examine their relationship with the facility. Family members strengthened by the group were able to present themselves as a source of support to the family members of new residents. Finally, family members were able to deal more successfully with their resident-relatives as a result of the support they received.

REFERENCES

Brubaker T.H. and E. Brubaker (1984). "Family Support of Older Persons in the Long-Term Care Setting: Recommendations for Practice." In W. H. Quinn and G. A. Hughston (eds.) *Independent Aging: Family and Social System Perspectives.* Rockville, Md.: Aspen Systems Corporation, in Press.

Blenkner, M. (1965). "The Normal Dependencies of Aging." Pp. 27–37 in R. Kalish (ed.), *The Dependencies of Old People.* Detroit: Institute of Gerontology, University of Michigan-Wayne State University.

Cohen, P.M. (1983). "A Group Approach for Working with Families of the Elderly." *The Gerontologist* 23:248–250.

Getzel, G. (1983). "Group Work with Kin and Friends Caring for the Elderly." *Social Work with Groups* 2:91–102.

Hartford, M.E. and R. Parsons (1982). "Short-Term Counseling Groups for People with Elderly Parents." *The Gerontologist* 19:394–398.

Numerof, R. (1983). "Building and Maintaining Bridges: Meeting the Psychosocial

Needs of Nursing Home Residents and Their Families." *Clinical Gerontologist* 1(4):53–67.

Springer, D.M. and Brubaker, T.H. (1984). *Family Caregivers and Dependent Elderly: Minimizing Stress and Maximizing Independence.* Beverly Hills: Sage Publications.

Streib, G.F. (1972). "Older Families and Their Troubles: Familial and Social Responses." *The Family Coordinator* 21:5–19.

Sussman, M.B. (1977). "Family Bureaucracy and The Elderly Individual: An Organizational/Linkage Perspective." In E. Shanas and M.B. Sussman (eds.) *Family, Bureaucracy and the Elderly.* Durham, North Carolina: Duke University Press.

Szafranski, L.M. (1984). "Using Patients as Co-Leaders." Pp. 132–140 in I. Burnside (ed.) *Working With the Elderly: Group Processes and Techniques.* Monterey, California: Wadsworth.

Assessing Caregiver Information Needs: A Brief Questionnaire

Linda J. Simonton, MSW

ABSTRACT. The type of information needed by caregivers of Alzheimer patients will vary, depending upon the stage of the caregiver's emotional acceptance of the illness and on the patient's condition. A brief questionnaire was developed to identify caregiver information needs.

The enormous adjustments that caregivers of Alzheimer patients must make have become increasingly well known. Recent investigations (George and Gwyther, 1983) have documented the changes in physical health, mental health, social participation, and financial status which are faced by caregivers of Alzheimer patients. Reasons for caregivers' feelings of burden have also been studied (Zarit, Reever, and Bach-Peterson).

The progressive nature of Alzheimer's Disease means that the patient's intellectual capacity, functional ability, and personality will change over time. The caregiver's adjustment to this decline will also be progressive. Bobbie Glaze (1982), one of the founders of the Alzheimer's Disease and Related Disorders Association, describes this adjustment as a mourning process, like "a funeral that never ends." Mental health researchers (Teusink and Mahler, 1984) have further observed that caregivers appear to go through stages of denial, overinvolvement, anger, guilt, and acceptance during the course of the Alzheimer patient's illness.

Linda J. Simonton is a Researcher in Clinical Gerontology, Younker Gerontology Project, Iowa Methodist Medical Center, 1200 Pleasant, Des Moines, IA 50308. She is a founder of the Alzheimer's Disease and Related Disorders Association of Des Moines.

177

The stage of their emotional acceptance will influence the type of information that caregivers need at any given time. The patient's condition will also be a determining factor. The literature (Hayter, 1982) suggests that generally, caregivers most frequently have concerns about the cause of the disease, heredity, the patient's physical appearance, a desire for contact with other interested persons, and a wish to contribute to education and research. Management of behavior problems associated with Alzheimer's Disease has also been identified as a source of caregiver stress about which information may be requested (Sanford, 1975).

To ensure that caregivers' needs for information are appropriately met, the Caregiver Information Guide in Table 1 was designed by the multi-disciplinary staff of a clinic specializing

TABLE 1

CAREGIVER INFORMATION GUIDE

Please let us know how important it is for us to answer the following questions for you.

	High Importance				Low Importance
How much can we expect the patient to do for themselves?	1	2	3	4	5
Has everything possible been done to find out if the patient's symptoms are treatable?	1	2	3	4	5
How can we help the patient to best use their abilities?	1	2	3	4	5
What is the cause of the patient's symptoms?	1	2	3	4	5
What can we do about certain behaviors that may cause problems (like false ideas, agitation, not eating, forgetting, hiding things, etc.)	1	2	3	4	5
Should the patient move to a higher level of care (i.e., from home to nursing home or from one level or nursing care to another?	1	2	3	4	5
What community services such as home health aids, sitters, or day care are available for the patient?	1	2	3	4	5
Does the patient need a guardian, conservator, or other legal protection?	1	2	3	4	5
What is the patient's life expectancy?	1	2	3	4	5
How can our family best come to an agreement over how to care for the patient?	1	2	3	4	5
Are the patient's medications correct?	1	2	3	4	5
Can the patient's illness be inherited by other family members?	1	2	3	4	5
What financial assistance is available to help pay for the patient's care?	1	2	3	4	5
What recreational or social activities would be best for the patient?	1	2	3	4	5
What can we expect the future course of the patient's illness to be?	1	2	3	4	5

in the diagnosis and management of Alzheimer's Disease. The brief questionnaire was based on the literature (Hayter, 1982; Teusink and Mahler, 1984) and on staff members' informal observations of the concerns expressed by caregivers who came to the clinic during its first year and a half of operation. Wording of the questions was deliberately kept simple, direct, and practical in tone so as to be easily understood by all caregivers.

The questionnaire, which is mailed to the caregiver and returned to the clinic prior to the initial clinic visit, has enabled staff to direct more in-depth attention to the special areas of concern noted by the caregiver. It has also helped staff to address issues which previously were often not directly brought up by caregivers in unstructured interviews, probably because of their emotional implications, i.e., the patient's life expectancy. Questions which caregivers do not identify as currently important, perhaps due to denial or to the fact that the patient has not yet progressed to that stage of the illness, can be addressed in subsequent visits.

Although the questionnaire was designed for use in a diagnostic clinic, it could also be used by:

1. Facilitators of caregiver support groups, to identify topics for program meetings.
2. Professionals who are providing counseling to family caregivers, to periodically assess caregiver concerns.
3. Social workers in hospitals, long term care facilities, adult day care programs, and home health agencies, to assist in referring family caregivers to other community services.

In a disease such as Alzheimer's, which affects so many aspects of the individual's life, the information presented to caregivers is crucial. The Caregiver Information Guide can assist professionals to provide the type of information caregivers most need and can emotionally accept.

REFERENCES

George, L.K., and Gwyther, L. Family caregivers of Alzheimer patients: correlates of burden and the impact of self-help groups. *Final Report to AARP,* December, 1983.

Glaze, B. One woman's story. *Journal of Gerontological Nursing,* 1982, *8,* 67–68.

Hayter, J. Helping families of patients with Alzheimer's Disease. *Journal of Gerontological Nursing,* 1982, *8,* 81–86.

Sanford, J. R. A. Tolerance of debility in elderly dependents by supporters at home. *British Medical Journal,* 1975, *3,* 471–473.

Teusink, J. P., and Mahler, S. Helping families cope with Alzheimer's Disease. *Hospital and Community Psychiatry,* 1984, *35,* 152–156.

Zarit, S., Reever, K., and Bach-Peterson, J. Relatives of the impaired elderly: correlates of feelings of burden. *The Gerontologist,* 1980, *20,* 649–655.

BOOK REVIEWS

YOUR PARENT'S KEEPER: A HANDBOOK OF PSY-
CHIATRIC CARE FOR THE ELDERLY. J.D. Lieff. *Cambridge, Mass: Ballinger Publishing Co., 1984, 284pp., $32.00.*

The lack of awareness about aging by clinical practitioners
and an unwillingness to work with this population has made
the psychiatric treatment of older people a difficult problem.
Books such as Butler and Lewis's *Aging and Mental Health*
and T.L. Brink's *Geriatric Psychotherapy,* however, have
done much to reconcile this disparity.

*Your Parent's Keeper: A Handbook of Psychiatric Care for
the Elderly* is a worthwhile and important resource for practitioners and educators who work with the elderly. The book is
also a useful and informative resource for those living and/or
caring for an elderly parent in need of help because of psychiatric difficulty.

The book advocates a team approach to psychiatric intervention with the elderly, and the author provides many examples and case histories of success using the team approach
to intervention. The book is written in the form of a handbook. Chapters can be read for specific information, or the
entire book can be read for an overview of the field of geriatric psychiatry. The last section of the book contains a number
of case histories which outline the team treatment approach
to care and are illustrative of many geriatric psychiatric problems facing older people.

The five specific units in the book contain chapters describing different perspectives to understanding and treating the
complex psychiatric problems of older people. The first unit

181

describes major cultural issues such as the widespread prejudice against treating psychiatric problems in the elderly, the overuse of medication by many elderly people, and the struggle to develop programs to treat needy patients. The author also provides an excellent overview of the physical and mental health research of older people.

The second unit provides an outline of the field of geriatric psychiatry including the major diagnoses and their treatments. Specific chapters include a look at depression, mania, dementia, psychosis and paronoia, anxiety, sleep disorders, reaction to medical illness and psychoparmacology principles. While each chapter provides a wealth of information about the particular issue and treatment modalities recommended, the chapters on depression, dementia and sleep disorders are of particular high quality.

The third unit of the book describes the format of the author's own problem-oriented, multimodal therapy treatment plan and the function of therapeutic teams. Each chapter describes a particular facet of the development of the geropsychiatric program, including implementation in a nursing home setting, a home psychiatric program, an acute general hospital unit and at a public health hospital.

The fourth unit includes twenty-seven case histories which portray the intricacies of evaluation and treatment. These cases provide the reader with an array of psychiatric problems facing older people and the various multimodal treatments used in working with them. The clinician may not always agree with the treatment plan, but the team approach provides an outlet for the kinds of interaction that make treatment more meaningful and manageable.

The last unit examines the future changes that could most affect the field of geriatric psychiatry. Three chapters make up this unit and describe the issues involved in training therapists, nurses and physicians, the politics of geropsychiatry and the role of high technology in the future of geriatrics.

The book is an excellent overview of the many issues that face clinicians working with older people. It is a handbook that should be included on bookshelves at clinics, hospitals, and nursing homes as well as in private practice settings. It provides good, solid research-supported facts and treatment approaches in working with this population.

The book is a must-read for those working in clinical settings with older people. It is a worthwhile and important reference for therapists and nurses, advanced students of counseling and family therapy, as well as the advanced gerontology student interested in geropsychiatry. It is a timely and well written resource that will be an important addition to your collection in years to come.

Robert A. Famighetti, MA
Assistant Professor and
Director of Gerontology
Kean College of New Jersey

FACING DEATH: PATIENTS, FAMILIES, AND PROFESSIONALS. A. Stedeford. Heinemann Medical, 1984.

Facing Death: Patients, Families, and Professionals is a comprehensive manual for the health care professional interested in expanding his knowledge of the death experience. Case histories and supporting material are taken from a survey conducted on a continuing care unit of a general hospital, the Sir Michael Sobell House in Oxford, England. Forty-one research couples were questioned by the author about all aspects of their illness. Their honest and revealing answers combined with the author's insight and experience produces an interesting book.

Chapters One through Three provide a case history for discussion with special attention to communication between patient-family-staff. The American reader will notice cultural differences in the discussion of the patient-doctor relationship and in the health-care delivery strategies. Chapter Four discusses the pitfalls of withholding information from patients and families with excellent case examples. Chapter Five discusses "dying trajectories" with an interesting differentiation in the emotional courses the psyche can take depending on one's knowledge about and expectation of death. The careful thought given to this chapter was an indication of the author's precision in exploring the complex subject of death.

Chapters Six through Nine cover a wide range of topics including the psychological response to physical symptoms such as pain, anorexia, breathlessness, weakness, and paralysis. The term treatment approach is strongly supported by the author. He points out in a discussion of psychological problems associated with treatment that members of the health care team other than the doctor may be in the best position to hear and give some types of information to the patient. Fears associated with dying were delineated into biological fears, separation anxiety, existential fear, fear of pain, and loss of control. Denial, anger, grief, and acceptance are described with an emphasis on the positive nature of psychological defenses.

Adjustment reactions to life-threatening illness are discussed in Chapter Ten. Problems involving communication and dependency are explored. The author advises that depression and anxiety are better treated with therapy than with psychotropic medications. Chapters Eleven through Fifteen discuss the detrimental use of psychological defenses including anxiety, depression, confusion, and paranoid reactions. The explanation of confusion and its etiology is especially helpful in its format and case examples are excellent.

Generally, this book could be a valuable text for courses on death and dying and an excellent addition to the library of any health care personnel. The author's observations are grounded in reality and bespeak an extremely sensitive and compassionate therapist.

Susan D. Henry, LCSW
Director, Dept. of Social Work
St. Vincent
Little Rock AR